Lutherans and the Challenge of Religious Pluralism

Edited by
Frank W. Klos, C. Lynn Nakamura,
and Daniel F. Martensen

AUGSBURG MINNEAPOLIS

LUTHERANS AND THE CHALLENGE OF RELIGIOUS PLURALISM

Cover design: Lecy Design

Library of Congress Cataloging-in-Publication Data

Lutherans and the challenge of religious pluralism / edited by Frank W. Klos, C. Lynn Nakamura, and Daniel F. Martensen.
p. cm.
Includes bibliographical references.
ISBN 0-8066-2453-1
1. Lutheran Church—North America. 2. Christianity and other religions. 3. Religious pluralism—Christianity. 4. Sociology, Christian (Lutheran). 5. Lutheran Church—Relations. 6. Lutheran Church—Doctrines. I. Klos, Frank W., 1924- II. Nakamura, C. Lynn, 1956- III. Martensen, Daniel F.
BX8041.L86 1989
284.1'73—dc20 89-36362
CIP

The paper used in this publication meets the minimum requirements of American National Standard for Information Sciences—Permanence of Paper for Printed Library Materials, ANSI Z329.48-1984. ∞™

Manufactured in the U.S.A. AF 9-2453
94 93 92 91 90 1 2 3 4 5 6 7 8 9 10

Contents

Preface

In her classic study of seashore life, *The Edge of the Sea*, Rachel Carson marvels at a bright, grass-green mollusk she discovered in a quiet Florida bay. Its closest living relatives inhabit the Indian Ocean. For Carson, this was one more exciting example of sea creatures that had come to inhabit North American waters and shores from some distant place.

Reflecting on this phenomenon, Carson wrote:

> And so transport and wide dispersal are a continuing universal process—an expression of the need of life to reach out and occupy all habitable parts of the earth. In any age the pattern is set by the shape of the continents and the flow of the currents; but it is never final, never completed.

This could be a provocative parable of the spread around the earth of the great religious faiths of mankind. Apart from the religious traditions of indigenous Native North Americans, all others found their way to this continent from Europe, from the Middle East, from India, from China and from Japan. History describes the pattern, ever-changing, that brought immigrants with their varying beliefs and practices to shape and reshape the communities where they settled. The "flow of the currents" today—educational opportunities, global business involvements, refuge from political strife, asylum from terrorism—demonstrate that the story is far from completed or even predictable.

Lutherans in the United States and Canada are well aware that their societies have become multiracial, multilifestyle and multireligious. What does this mean for us as thoughtful, committed followers of Jesus Christ? How do we build friendly, healthy relationships with neighbors who have differing faiths from our own?

This book of essays seeks to deal with these and related questions in ways that will encourage congregations to reach out in friendship to members of other faiths living in their communities. Friendship can lead to the formation of dialogue groups promoting mutual understanding and acceptance. It can also foster joint efforts to deal with local social issues and ecological concerns. Without compromising our Christian convictions, we can forge bonds of trust and respect with people who are Muslims, Buddhists, Hindus, Shintoists. As we do so we may realize more intensely that, in the words of Francis of Assisi, we are "all creatures of our God and king."

The place to begin in any journey of new understandings and actions is with basics. In "Thinking about Religion and Religions," Roland E. Miller explores the nature of religion and the unique way the major world faiths lay claim to being the religion for all people. As Miller explains the fundamental teachings of each faith tradition, he seeks to formulate what he calls its "core intuition." A core intuition is simply a few words or phrases that distill complicated beliefs and practices to find the essence and motivating power of a particular faith heritage.

Wi Jo Kang pays particular attention to the concept of community in "The Christian Church and the Neighbors of Asian Faiths." Learning to know and accept those who represent the great faiths of Asia involves becoming familiar with the special sense of community that undergirds each. Over time, customs and teachings have become intertwined, forming a cultural mosaic. Being able to discuss similarities and differences of competing faiths within Asia requires respect for the customs they treasure in community life.

For Christians, faith is built solidly on the person and work of Jesus Christ. Gospel accounts proclaim that he is the only way to God. Small wonder that Paul described Christ as "folly to the Greeks and a stumbling block to the Jews." However, there seems to be some form of respect for Jesus in the major faiths being considered. "The Identity and Meaning of Jesus Christ in the Dialogue with World Religions," by Carl E. Braaten is an examination and analysis of that respect. Braaten also surveys the wide variety of Christian understandings of who Jesus was and what he did on behalf of a sinful humanity to reconcile individuals with a loving and just God. Against this shifting background, Braaten suggests that new thought forms may be necessary to help followers of other faiths know that God, in Christ, has much to offer them in their quest for truth.

Paul Sponheim tackles the truth issue forthrightly and profoundly. His essay, "The Truth Will Make You Free," probes the reality of the Christian's confidence that through Jesus Christ God "was reconciling the world to himself." With philosophical rigor and theological conviction, Sponheim studies the nature of truth and tests its integrity. Further, he considers ways the truth question must be handled in dialogues with members of other world faiths who also claim ultimate truth for their belief structures.

The last essay, "What Then Shall We Do?" by Paul V. Martinson, deals with the practical aspects of interactive dialogue encounters that Christians may have with members of other world religions. He discusses the challenges, the risk-taking, and the benefits of friendly bridge-building among groups that have such divergent religious backgrounds. Martinson offers some perceptive insights into the contributions intentional dialogues can make to the future of a troubled planet ripe for healing renewal.

Frank W. Klos

Contributors

Carl E. Braaten	Professor, Systematic Theology, Lutheran School of Theology at Chicago, Chicago, Illinois
Wi Jo Kang	Professor, World Missions, Wartburg Theological Seminary, Dubuque, Iowa
Paul Varo Martinson	Professor, Christian Missions and World Religions, Luther Northwestern Theological Seminary, St. Paul, Minnesota
Roland E. Miller	Academic Dean and Professor, Religious Studies, Luther College, University of Regina, Regina, Saskatchewan
Paul R. Sponheim	Professor, Systematic Theology, Luther Northwestern Theological Seminary, St. Paul, Minnesota

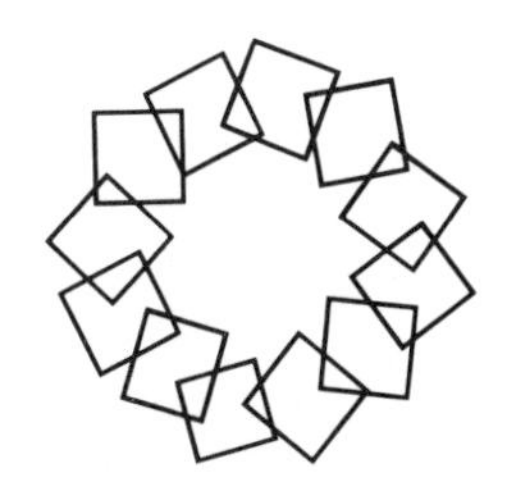

1

RELIGION AND RELIGIONS

Roland E. Miller

Is it possible to identify and explain the central ideas of the major world religions?

Why bother? Many Christians may wonder why they should spend time thinking about other religions of humanity. One of the compelling answers is located right in Mainville, USA. Have you visited Mainville recently? If you have, you will note that it is religiously different from what it used to be.

The citizens of Mainville were accustomed to some variety in their community's religious life. On the town square there were three churches—Congregational, Methodist, and Presbyterian. The Baptist, Catholic, and Lutheran churches were just down adjoining streets. A Jewish synagogue had been established in the town for many years. After a while, Seventh-Day Adventists and Mormons came along and rocked the boat a little. But there was nothing to compare with the current scene.

Sectarian Christian groups have proliferated. Now Muslims, Hindus, Buddhists, and Sikhs have come to Mainville in considerable numbers. Some are students at Central College. Others are refugees. They are professional people; workers in restaurants, hospitals, and new industrial plants; and those employed in service jobs. Most of them have come on successive waves of immigration, as Mainville grew in size and prosperity. Generally Mainville citizens have accepted these new arrivals in a cordial way. They have found the newcomers to be hard-working and well-behaved contributors to the life of the community.

Almost without realizing it, the small city of Mainville has become an international community.

Religious pluralism is therefore an obvious reality. Mainville can no longer be regarded as a "one-religion" town, or as a totally Christian community. While not all of these new citizens seem particularly interested in their traditional religions, many of them are fervent in their faith and practice. Last month, for example, the *Mainville Daily Herald* announced the dedication of a new Muslim mosque! Mainville, USA, is religiously different from what it used to be.

Today almost all of us are living in some Mainville or other! This fact raises some serious questions, many quite familiar to Christian believers in areas of the world called "mission fields."

- How are differing religions to be judged in the light of the saving intention of God's redemptive work in Christ? In what sense is God near to Buddhists, Hindus, and Muslims?
- If these people are ordinary, good citizens, does it not imply that their religion is in some sense good? What do they believe? What is their hope?
- Is it really important to proclaim the gospel to people like these? What does the gospel give that they do not have? Where is our starting point? What do we share Christ meaningfully with them?

These questions and others like them are being asked today by thoughtful Christians. One thing seems obvious and clear. Christians who want to deal intelligently with these issues, who want to understand their faith in relation to other faiths, and who are concerned to share the gospel with all their neighbors, must have a better-than-average knowledge of the major religions of the world. How can this knowledge be obtained, when the field is so vast and the issues so profound? We can at least make a small beginning in providing some starting points for Mainville Christians who are thinking about religion and religions.

RELIGION

Since there are so many religions in the world, perhaps the best way to begin is to examine religion in the singular. Of course, one can start with either religion or religions, but neither approach is simple. Think of discussing "sport" and "sports." At first, the singular term "sport" seems simpler, but when you try to define it, it is hard to be precise. On the other hand, the plural "sports" is also complicated because it includes so much, everything from basketball to free-style skiing. The same holds true with "religion" and "religions." The former is so hard to define and the latter is so inclusive. Let us, however, begin with the singular.

A problem we encounter at once is that in everyday language the word *religion* is used quite loosely. In popular speech, it is even used as a synonym for "denomination." In this way religion is sometimes made equivalent to affiliation with a Christian organization. For instance, if someone asks another person "What's your religion?" the other may reply "I'm a Lutheran!" Yet Lutheranism is only one stream that feeds into the religion of Christianity, and Christianity in turn is only one of the religions of the world. This kind of inexact use of the term religion complicates the task of examining its meaning. But it also points to a truth: "Religion" is a composite term that attempts to capture and sum up both individual experiences of many particular human beings and also universal experiences of all human beings.

Undeniably, there is a force called religion surging through the history of humanity. Its marks are everywhere on the sands of human history. Opinions may differ about that force, but no one can deny that it is there. Religion has produced the noblest monuments and the finest works of art known to humanity. It has propelled men and women into mighty movements, called forth immense expenditures of energy, and inspired all-but-impossible sacrifices. It has expressed itself in many diverse forms, ranging from the great world religions to more localized ethnic and tribal forms and to smaller sects. Despite the dilution of its influence in modern times, religion still remains as the primary source of human ideals, the major power that motivates behavior, and the hope of life for most individuals in the world today.

When we use the word "religion," all of us have a sense of what it implies, even though no one can put it into words in a way that fully satisfies. Many people have tried to define religion, but no single definition has won the day. That is hardly surprising. Like "art" and "beauty," its meaning is very much in the eye of the beholder.

It is more useful to identify the ways of defining religion than to look for a single perfect definition. There are at least three possibilities. In the first place, we may define the term quite broadly. For example, we may say that a person's religion is what he or she puts first in life. It is common to hear someone comment, "His religion is politics," or "Her religion is money." When Martin Luther explained the First Commandment with the words: "We should fear, love and trust in God above all things," he was suggesting that your god is what you put first in your life. According to this view, almost anything can become religion. Paradoxically, even Marxism may be viewed as a religion, even though it rejects religion! But if religion is everything, is it anything?

Secondly, we may also define religion narrowly. We can try to get closer to its essential element. This approach assumes that there is such an essential element in religious experience that distinguishes it from all other human experiences and behavior. That essential element is what most people call "the experience of God." From this point of view, religion has a unique quality. It has to do with Something or Someone beyond. Scholars search for the proper word for that "Someone" or "Something." Many feel that because all faiths must be included under the definition, a neutral term such as "The Sacred," "The Ultimate," "The Holy," "The Mystery," "The Power," "The Focus," "The Wholly Other," is preferable to the word "God." From this perspective we might define religion as "the experience of the Sacred, and the feelings, beliefs, and practices that arise from that experience." Those who take this approach argue strongly that the word religion cannot be used for anything or for everything!

Finally, we may define religion theologically, that is, from the perspective of our faith. The "our" refers to the faith of the believer, whatever that religion might be. Neutrality is not a consideration here, but rather the faith commitment of the believer. Every religion will have its own theology of religion, its own view of what the existence of religion implies. From the Christian point of view that which some call "The Sacred" or "The Ultimate" is none other than the living God who is revealed in nature, in human conscience, and in the biblical revelation. The living God not only stands over against all else but is also engaged with every human being, with holy demand and loving grace, causing both trembling and attraction. The human response to that engagement with God is what we call religion.

This leads to a possible theological definition of religion that some Christians might use in the light of biblical teaching. Religion is humanity's search for God and rebellion against God. The definition implies that all humans have a relationship with God, but that relation is an ambivalent one. On the one hand, humanity is conscious of God and seeks for a true relation with the Lord. On the other hand, that search is also frustrated by human weakness and corruption. This paradox explains the positive and negative aspects of religion, its glory and its tragedy. It is at the same time a movement toward God and a movement away from God. "Religion is humanity's flight to God, and flight from God."[1] Theological definitions such as these are helpful to Christians not only for their understanding of other religions in the light of Christian faith, but also for their understanding of the Christian religion itself.

One possible conclusion to be drawn from what we have said is that all three ways of defining religion in the singular can help us to understand our Mainville neighbors. To review, in the broad sense religion refers to one's primary allegiance in life; in the narrow sense, it refers to one's spiritual experience of that which is regarded as Ultimate and to the expressions of that experience; and, in the theological sense, it refers to humanity's encounter and relation with the living God, as revealed in the Scriptures. It is clear that the members of other religions in Mainville are religious in every one of these three ways. First of all, they have a primary allegiance. Secondly, they testify to an experience of reality that spiritually controls their lives. Thirdly, recognized or unrecognized, they have a relationship with the living God, who desires all to be saved and to come to the knowledge of the truth.

A second conclusion may be drawn. It is not so crucial to be able to define the word religion as it is to be deeply aware of that universal, fundamental, and powerful drive in human beings that produces religions. The drive is the impulse to draw near to God. St. Paul traces that spiritual instinct to the very creative act of God, who "gives to all life and breath and everything. . . . that they should seek God, in the hope that they might feel after him and find him" (Acts 17:25, 27). The religious instinct or consciousness is God's special grace to people, the gifting of the essence of humanity and a basis for fellowship with the divine, which lifts them above the category of animal. It is against this background that we must view our friends in Mainville's new religions, as we share with them what we have learned from "a man whom he has appointed" (Acts 17:31).

THE RELIGIONS OF HUMANITY

While not without its value, as we have seen, the discussion of the word "religion" in the singular does not take us very far in explaining the particular central idea of Hindus, Buddhists, Jews, or Muslims. We must draw nearer to our Mainville neighbors than we have done so far. Let us therefore leave religion in the singular and consider religions in the plural. Here, we might assume, is something easier. After all, a specific religion is concrete, visible, describable. Can we not see the mosque on the corner of Second and Main? Can we not watch our neighbors taking off their shoes as they enter? Can we not hear their call to prayer? Can we not observe them praying in airports as we travel? Here is something easier, men and women like ourselves, brothers and sisters in a common human family residing in the same earthly village and doing some of the things that we do. This we will be able to understand. Let us see how they are "feeling after" God, and then let us try to understand our responsibility toward them!

It would be unrealistic, however, not to recognize that here too we face a formidable task: First of all, we are dealing with huge religious systems. Secondly, in many ways they are different in their beliefs and customs, and seem strange. Thirdly, since the faith of another human being is a very personal and private thing, it is to some extent inaccessible to nonparticipants. Recognizing the existence of such difficulties, nevertheless let us go forward in what can be an exciting and rewarding venture.

The religions of humanity! Where do we begin? We can start by listing some of the major religions of the world and noting their size:[2]

■ Christians	1,684,544,500
■ Muslims	880,680,000
■ Hindus	674,564,600
■ Buddhists	316,301,000
■ Chinese religions	193,201,026
■ Jews	18,429,100
■ Sikhs	17,017,000
■ Tribal religions	99,201,600

The list could be extended since there are many smaller religions, and since new ones are constantly being formed. One authority estimates that 113,454,200 people fall into his category of "new" religions.[3] Most persons will probably acknowledge that there are some important religions, past and present, whose names they do not know. Listing religious populations does remind us of the great diversity of opinion that exists and the immensity of the task Christians face, both in understanding others and in communicating the gospel. However, such a listing does not get us closer to religious believers themselves.

Another way of beginning is to attempt to classify the religions. They are frequently divided into groups. By some they are divided into two major streams called Eastern and Western. The Eastern stream, it is suggested, includes Hinduism, Buddhism, Confucianism, and others. The Western stream includes Judaism, Christianity, and Islam. Other scholars hold that it is more accurate to speak of three major streams: the Semitic stream, which includes Judaism, Christianity, and Islam; the Indian stream, which includes Jainism, Hinduism, and Buddhism; and the Chinese stream, which includes Confucianism,

Taoism, and others. Finally, there is another important stream called "primal" or "tribal" religions (older terms were "animistic," or "preliterate," or "primitive" religions). Whatever the division, these major streams pour in the bulk of the waters that make up the great river of religion running through human life.

Classifying religions helps us to some extent. For example, let us consider the division between Semitic and Indian religion. The Semitic stream says that there is a distinction between God and humanity, between Creator and creature. God and human beings are different. They are two dimensions of reality, not to be confused. True religion depends on setting up the correct relation between God and humanity. The Indian stream suggests another basic view: God and human beings are not separate. Rather, the divine soul and the human soul are essentially one. True religion means becoming aware of this reality and overcoming the false sense of separation.

Clearly a fundamental issue is involved in these two contrasting positions. The goals, beliefs, and practices of a religion are in part determined by its approach to this fundamental issue. Classifying religions, therefore, does give us some assistance in thinking through what is going on in the individual religions. However, such classification has at least two problems. First of all, it paints with too broad a brush. Secondly, it does not deal seriously enough with the convictions of religious believers themselves, who regard their own religions as uniquely different from others. Let us look more closely at the latter issue and consider the hard question of whether Christianity is *a* religion that can be classified and compared with others.

True believers seldom appreciate having their religion listed with other religions. This makes it appear that their faith has only relative value, a kind of "new improved detergent that makes clothes whiter." That picture is unacceptable. For believers, their faith is absolute. No matter what outsiders may think about it, their religion, at least in the ideal sense, is perfect. In seeing Christianity on a list with other religions, a Christian might even strenuously object: "Is there not a continental divide that separates the streams of religion? After all, Christianity flows in one direction, and all other religions flow in another direction.

The religions of humanity should be divided into two groups: Christianity and all others!"

The solution to this issue may be to recognize that Christianity has two sides. It is both a religion and a special religion. The first side emphasizes that it is, in fact, *a* religion. It has all the marks of a religion. It has beliefs and practices which we can describe. It has in its long history a bewildering variety of groups and viewpoints which we can study. It is composed of ordinary human beings with all their quirks and foibles. It has its ups and downs, good moments and bad moments. It has organizations and buildings, programs and activities. It is a human construction, of the earth, earthy. People of other faiths look at Christianity and see *a* religion. Because it is *a* religion it can be listed, grouped, and compared.

But Christianity has another side, a special one, that only Christians who look at it through the eyes of faith can see. Christians know, or should know, that there is a difference between the religion of Christianity and the gospel. It is Jesus Christ, not Christianity, who is the Way, the Truth and the Life. Christians are also aware that as a religion Christianity is under judgment. That judgment comes, in part, from the world around us. Why is it that Jesus Christ is universally respected, but in many parts of the world Christianity is disliked and rejected? At least some of the fault must be laid at the door of Christianity, for it is a very imperfect image, and at times a caricature, of its Lord. Judgment also comes from the sensitized conscience of Christians who confess with Paul, on behalf of the whole church as well as for themselves: "I am the chief of sinners." Nevertheless, despite its admitted faults, Christians regard their religion as having a special quality and a special role. As the people of faith, it is the Spirit-produced response to the saving revelation of God. And as the people of commitment, it is the bearer of God's gift and herald of good news. Christians are God's forgiven and enlivened people, who are in the world that they may declare the wonderful deeds of the One who called us out of darkness into marvelous light.

Having said this, it is also well to recognize that Muslims similarly regard Islam as incomparable. Hindus regard Hinduism the same way. On the surface, one claim seems to be as strong as the other. What shall we conclude from this? It is clear that we must move beyond claims to meaning, beyond affirmations of uniqueness based on classifications, to questions of content. What does the religion of Islam proclaim? What does Hinduism say? What does Buddhism stand for? It is clear that we must consider each religion in and for itself. We must seek to understand each religion's central theme or themes, and at the same time be sure that we grasp the corresponding insight of the Christian faith. Through this kind of process Christians of Mainville can advance in their effort to develop an appropriate attitude and approach toward people of other faiths.

CORE INTUITIONS

Before speeding forward, it is good to note a caution sign on this road: "Proceed slowly and carefully." Within each religion there exists a great diversity of positions and points of view. Christians above all can appreciate the problem of diversity. Not only are there many denominations, but every denomination has its inner divisions. It has even been suggested that there are as many "Christianities" in the world as there are individual Christians.[4] What Christians may not fully realize, however, is that other religions also contain denominational variety. There are distinct differences between: Saivism and Vaishnavism in Hindu faith; Theravada and Zen in Buddhist faith; Sunni and Shi'a in Muslim faith; Orthodox, Conservative, and Reform in Jewish faith. Not only are there many definable groups among other religions, but also within each group there can be submovements and strong personal differences of opinion. The multiplicity of viewpoints that exists within each religious tradition means that "studying each religion in and for itself" is not as simple and straightforward as it first seems.

Yet, existence of a variety of different views does not eliminate the reality of a common center. Just as "Christianity" and "Christian" are terms that do stand for something, so also "Islam" and "Muslim" mean something. Surely there is such a common element or elements in Christianity that makes it more than the sum total of its parts. Like rolling thunder, the great ecumenical creeds of the church sound forth their message from the past. And the prophetic voices of universally respected Christian teachers declare "Here I stand!", evoking the echoing response, "Here we too stand!" Professor Sarvepalli Radhakrishnan, Indian philosopher and statesman, once said that religion is an "insight into reality."[5] We might modify his famous definition to say, "A religion is an insight into reality." What is that insight, that golden thread that holds together the tapestry of faith, that dominant theme in the music which Christians make to the Lord in their hearts? Christians sense what it is for them. Can they sense the same for others?

This, then, is my task. I am seeking out that basic element which is distinctive in each religion, which is regarded by its adherents as central to their faith, and from which the practical expressions of their religion emerge.

A religion looks like a great oak tree with its mass of branches and leaves. Each leaf could represent some facet of that religion's belief or practice, each branch some movement within that religion. Yet within the branches and leaves, sometimes hidden but always there, is the trunk flowing with life-giving sap, a trunk which supports the whole and the root from which everything stems. What is that root and trunk? Said differently, what is the originating fountain or beating heart, the central principle or core intuition, of each of the world's major religions that defines it and which inspires its members?

As one scholar noted, it is the central theme that gives continuity to all the expressions of a religion since "the understanding of this [theme] may, like a great key, unlock an otherwise strange-appearing world of experience."[6]

Not even the members of a religion, however, can always or easily answer the question: What is the dominant theme of your faith? Many believers feel their religion. They intuit the faith. They cannot describe it. If you ask them to state the core element, they might find the question difficult and perhaps become embarrassed or impatient. They are not explainers. They are believers, worshipers, and doers. Still other members of a religion might have trouble with the question because they have stopped feeling anything. They are nominal, marginalized religionists, who keep to the name of their religion, but with an interest only skin-deep. Asking them to describe the beating heart of the faith is not a profitable exercise. There are others, however, who can tell what they believe and why. They cannot express their feelings fully, and their tongues stammer before the Mystery. But no matter how stumbling the words, there is some expression of awe, some confession of faith, some explanation of meaning. What, then, do Jews, Muslims, Hindus, Buddhists, and Confucianists express, confess, and explain when they are asked about their religion?

JUDAISM

It is Saturday morning in Mainville. Some members of the local Jewish community are wending their way to the synagogue, "the place of assembly." The outside of the square stone building does not tell the casual observer very much. He or she has to go inside to feel the warm and friendly bustle. It is the Sabbath, the special day of the week for Jewish believers, the set apart day, a time for rest and rejoicing. The congregation is facing toward one wall, which marks the direction of Jerusalem. Against the wall is a box-like depository, the ark, which contains handwritten scrolls of the law of Moses, the Torah. Hanging in front of it is an "eternal light" that memorializes the altar in the first Temple and symbolizes the continuity of Jewish faith. The rabbi is about to begin the service. The reading stand is in a central place, for the highlight of the service will be the instruction from the Torah. The prayer books are ready: "Bless the Lord . . . May He cause His Kingdom to come . . . Hear O Israel, the Lord is our God, the Lord is One." The words seem to roll down from the centuries. "Hear, O Israel . . ." The congregation listens and responds with a deep sense of their unity with all the chosen people of the past. Across that spectrum of time, from Abraham to Golda Meir, what is it that Jews have been hearing and feeling?

It is not easy to put into words. There is a saying among Jews: "To be a Jew is to argue what it means to be a Jew." Perhaps the clue is in the prayer that sanctifies the wine at the Sabbath meal:

> For thou has chosen and sanctified us above all nations, in love and favour has given us thy holy Sabbath as an inheritance.[7]

Being chosen, being set apart, receiving God's love and favor, inheriting God's rest, all these ideas are keys to understanding the pulse of the Jewish heart.

The tree of Judaism seems less strange than other trees in the forest of religion. After all, the first part of Jewish history is well-known to Christians, who refer to it as "the Old Testament." The last part is also generally known, including the suffering of the Jews in the Holocaust in Europe and the story of modern Israel. There is, however, a problem with our lack of knowledge of what falls in between. The great middle of Judaism, which occupies the greatest portion of space in Jewish histories, is a mystery to most Christians.

There is another factor that hinders us from understanding Jews. Christians tend to view Jews as pre-Christians. Jews, on the other hand, view their religion as the full tree of life in the garden of humanity. Christians often think of Jews as people who have not perceived the true significance of their own history and message. Jews, on the other hand, think of themselves as God's select people who truly represent and communicate the divine intention for human life. Christians want to tell Jews what they should believe in the light of the Messiah, Jesus Christ. Jews want to tell Christians what they believe about the messianic age still to come. These differing viewpoints should give us some caution. A little reflection will convince us that it will be impossible for Christians to understand living Judaism unless they listen and let Jews tell us what they believe.

When we think of Judaism, we may think of many things. We may think of the wonder of Jewish identity and its capacity to survive. We may think of words like "kosher" (the official stamp of approval) and Jewish laws in general. We may think of well-known festivals: Hanukkah, the feast of lights, which celebrates the Jewish recovery of Jerusalem in 165 B.C.E.; Yom Kippur, the Day of Atonement, a time for fasting, prayer, and confession; Passover, the day of deliverance. We may think of the Scriptures of the Jews, the three parts of which they call the Torah, the Prophets, and the Writings. The word "Torah," however, is also used in a wider sense to include all the additional oral revelation that God has provided through Jewish teachers over the ages. An example of this sacred lore is the Talmud (sixty-three volumes!), a vast repository of rabbinical learning on which Jewish faith, law, and story feed. We may think of the doctrines that are so important in Judaism: creation, revelation, and redemption. Divisions might be noted such as: Orthodox, Conservative, Reconstructionist, and Reform. We may consider Jewish culture and learning: Maimonides and Einstein, Elie Wiesel and Isaac Stern. The photographs of Auschwitz or the current troubles in Israel may come to mind. Or we may think of our Jewish neighbors with whom we play bridge. When we think of Judaism, we think of many things.

Is there a trunk hidden beneath these luxuriant branches? Can we also think of a central idea in Jewish faith?

It is often suggested that the primary Jewish belief is monotheism. That, in a sense, is very true. Jews, however, do not traditionally think of the existence and the oneness of God as one doctrine on a list:

> God is neither a thing nor an idea; He is within and beyond all ideas. To think of Him is to open our minds to His all-pervading presence. To think of things means to have a concept within the mind, while to think of Him is like walking under a canopy of thought . . . He is not a being, whose existence could be either confirmed or described by our thoughts. He is a Reality, in the face of which, when becoming alive to its meaning, we are overtaken with a feeling of infinite unworthiness.[8]

When Abraham Heschel spoke these words he was rephrasing the basic instinct of Judaism that God is the living God and life is to be conducted in relation to that reality. It is said therefore that Judaism is "a way of life that endeavors to transform virtually every human action into a means of communion with God."[9]

We are approaching the trunk of the tree but must proceed a little farther. Other religions, too, may describe themselves as a way of life related to God. There is another word, however, a simple one, that carries us into the very heart of Jewish emotion. That word is belonging. Judaism is a celebration of belonging. It is a way of life that reflects and celebrates the Jewish sense of belonging to the living God. Words such as these might express the Jewish feeling: "We belong to God. God is our God. God has made us the people of God. Because we belong to God, we are obedient to God's will. We are chosen to obey it. God will bless those who are obedient. We belong to God."

This core intuition of Jewish religion can be expressed in many ways, but the essential thought runs clear through all the intricacies of Jewish religious life and history. The living God has chosen the people of Israel and has made an everlasting covenant with them. They bear God's name and can say our God. God has made the divine will known to them and has set them apart. They belong to God as no one else in the world. Belonging to God incorporates the elements of thankfulness, obedience, and hope. "O give thanks unto the Lord, for he is good; his steadfast love endures for-ever" (Ps. 118:1). "Thy word is a lamp to my feet and a light to my path. I have sworn an oath and confirmed it, to observe thy righteous ordinances" (Ps. 119:105-106). "O sing to the Lord a new song, for he has done marvelous things; His right arm and his holy arm have gotten him victory" (Ps. 98:1).

The theme of belonging runs through all the events of Jewish history, tying them together with a common thread.

- Call of Abraham: God promised that Abraham would be the father of a great nation, a people belonging to God, in a land that God would give to them.
- Exodus from Egypt: God delivered this people from the hands of their enemies with a mighty salvation. "I have remembered my covenant . . . I will redeem you with an out-stretched arm . . . I will take you for my people, and I will be your God" (Ex. 6:5-7).
- Giving of the Law: "You shall be holy, for I the Lord your God am holy" (Lev. 19:2). God revealed the divine will and set the behavior patterns for this set-apart people; henceforth, they must live as people who belong to God.

- Kingdom of David: God made it clear that those who belong to God and are true to God shall have blessings in this life—a land and a kingdom.
- Message of the prophets: Those who belong to God are warned that they have a corresponding responsibility to do the works of God, and moral failure will be punished. "You only have I known of all the families of the earth; *therefore* I will punish you for all your iniquities" (Amos 3:2).
- Exiles, diaspora, persecutions, holocaust, expulsion and degradation, restrictions and ghettos, persecution and massacre: For centuries Jews suffered them all. Where is God, they asked, and attributed the silence of God to their sins. Nevertheless, they affirmed their belonging in their confidence that some day God would redeem the people. "Next year Jerusalem!"
- Promise of the Messiah: For some Jews it means a wonderful, redeeming person; for others, a wonderful age of righteousness and joy. But for all Jews, the prayer for the coming of the Messiah is a prayer for deliverance for those who belong to God: "Hasten the advent of the Messianic redemption! Each and everyday we hope for Your deliverance. Praised are you, O Lord, who assures our deliverance!"[10]
- Land of Israel: In Jewish imagination and hope the sense of belonging is concretized and fulfilled in the land. The idea was there from the beginning, from Abraham's time itself: "And I will establish my covenant between me and you, and your descendants after you . . . for an everlasting covenant, to be God to you and to your descendants after you. And I will give to you, and to your descendants after you, the land of your sojournings, all the land of Canaan, for an everlasting possession" (Gen. 17:7-8).

The birth of the modern state of Israel drew together the elements of covenant, deliverance, sacred land, and job. In 1948, the United Nations created the nation-state of Israel from a portion of Palestine. Although the decision created immense problems, still unresolved, for Jews everywhere it confirmed the feeling that they belong to God. The new nation said to them that God keeps promises, and the loyalty of this people will be rewarded. The words of Psalm 126 (vv. 1-2) spoken in the grace after meals, now sounded forth with new meaning: "When the Lord restored the fortunes of Zion, we were like those who dream. Then our mouth was filled with laughter, and our tongue with shouts of joy." Complete joy would come only with the final restoration of the Temple. But the return to the promised land signaled to Jews everywhere that the Kaddish prayer which begins every Sabbath service has been and is being fulfilled:

> May the great Name of God be exalted and sanctified in the world which He created according to His will, and may He cause His Kingdom to come, in your lives and in your days, and in the lives of all the House of Israel; speedily, and in a short time. Amen.

The sense of belonging that characterizes Judaism raises two questions for Christians: "What is the Christian idea of belonging?" and "What is the good news in the gospel for Jews?"

ISLAM

It is now Friday noon in Mainville. Lunch counters are jammed and alive with conversation about the coming weekend. In the Muslim mosque at Smith and Lincoln, however, the weekend has already begun, for Friday noon is a central worship time for Muslims. While the Mainville mosque is not one of the great structures of the Islamic world, Mainville Muslims love to gather there. It is their fellowship hall and educational center. Far more important, however, it is the place of prayer for the believing community. The word "mosque" comes from the Arabic term *masjid*, which means "the place of prostration." You may have viewed that remarkable scene of Muslims praying and "remembering God."

As Muslims enter the mosque, they remove their shoes as a sign of respect. Near the entrance is an area for the washing of face, hands, and feet, a ritual purification that precedes prayer. Inside, the mosque is brightly lit, uncluttered in appearance, without pews but with many carpets, all designed to provide physical space and comfort for prayer. There are no images or pictures, but on the wall are inscribed some Arabic verses from the Qur'an, the sacred book of Islam. On one of the walls there is an indentation that marks the direction of the city of Mecca in Arabia, the direction in which to pray. There is also a small pulpit from which a short message will be delivered during the service. The Mainville mosque does not have minarets, those tall slender towers from which the call to prayer is uttered. Still, the call is heard by Mainville worshipers: "Come to salvation, come to prayer . . ." Before the prayer begins each one makes a declaration in the heart: "Now I intend to worship God." As the service unfolds, at a special moment, the worshipers fall to their knees and touch their foreheads to the floor, murmuring the words: "God is great, God is great . . ." That murmur is joined by millions of the faithful throughout the world, becoming the crescendo of faith that unites Muslim believers everywhere.

To penetrate the central core of Muslim religious devotion may not seem difficult to Christians who reverence God Almighty. There are, however, three special problems of which we must be aware as we begin the task of understanding Muslims. The first is the inadequate and often insensitive portrayal of Muslims in the news media today, which hinders the possibility of achieving empathy. The second is our awareness of the bad relations that have existed between Christians and Muslims in the past and still haunt the present. The third is the Muslim misunderstanding of the Christian faith, especially its primary teaching concerning Jesus Christ. Let us look briefly at each of these three problems.

The problem obvious to all is the distortion that is imprinted on everyday minds by half-minute television clips of burning planes and destroyed Beirut streets; or by the glowering visage of a now deceased, aged and angry religious leader in Iran, portrayed as representative of all Muslims.

Some of the distortions and fictions are relatively easy to overcome. For example, one fiction is that "All Muslims are Arab." The reality is that only about 15 percent of the Muslim world is Arab. Other distortions are more difficult to deal with. Another fiction is that "All Muslims are violent." The reality is that Muslims have among them the same range of personalities and emotions as any other human group. A third fiction is that "All Muslims support terrorism." The reality is that most Muslims distinguish between mindless violence, which they reject, and the principle of defensive warfare and the right to struggle for liberation, which they accept.

The problem of distortion is a contemporary extension of the second problem, the sorrowful history of bad relations between Christianity and Islam over a period of many centuries. While offset from time to time by noble examples of friendship, too often the interaction between the two religions has been abrasive and antagonistic in spirit. In the century following the birth of historical Islam (622 C.E.), aggressive Arab Muslim forces captured the major centers of Christianity in the Mediterranean world and advanced into Europe. Later, at the time of the Crusades, the situation was reversed. Christian knights under the auspices of the Church attempted forcefully to retake the Holy Land for Christendom, conducting a reign of terror in Christ's name. Soon the situation reversed again. During the period of the Reformation, the forces of the Muslim Ottoman Turks were invited into Europe by the Christian king of France, Francis I, who was playing politics against the Holy Roman Emperor, King Charles V of Spain. The Turks overran the Balkans and penetrated to Vienna, the very heart of Europe, before they were held in check. Finally, in modern times, Christians of the West invaded almost all the Muslim nations of the world, for imperial and economic reasons, and made them their colonies. Mutual distrust and often hatred were born from these events and live on today. Both sides suffer severely from the heritage of the past and from the caricatures of the present.

The third problem that hinders understanding of Islam stems from Muslim misunderstandings of the Christian faith. Many of these misunderstandings arose from Christian heresies and, ultimately, from Christian failure to communicate the gospel clearly and at the right time. Most Christians are startled to discover that Muslims believe that Christians are polytheists who worship three gods (Father, Son, and Mary). Muslims also are inclined to regard Christians as idolaters. They believe that Christians have taken a noble human being, Jesus the prophet, whom they call *'Isa Nabi*, and have raised him to the stature of God. Muslims are appalled by the phrase "Son of God," which to them implies the blasphemy that God has taken a wife. In addition, Muslims believe that Christians have even misunderstood aspects of the personal history of *'Isa Nabi*, the Messiah. He did not die on the cross, as Christians believe. Is he not God's chosen messenger-servant-sign, who is even called God's Word? Surely God would not allow such a one to suffer the defilement of a criminal's death! The truth is that God took Jesus directly to heaven, from where he will return in the last days to help establish God's kingdom and righteousness on earth. Thus Jesus has a high status in Islam and is a deeply respected figure. But from their view he does not participate in the being of God, nor does he have a saving function that is different from the other prophets sent by God, from Adam to Muhammad.

In view of these misunderstandings, it is clear that special attitudes and efforts are necessary for a Christian to gain entry into a Muslim heart. On the surface it would seem that Islam, next to Judaism, should be the easiest of religions for a Christian to consider and relate to. However, the history of failure suggests that the approach must be based on genuine understanding. At its best, this approach calls for a prayer for forgiveness and grace.

When we think of Islam, we may think of many things. We may think of our Indonesian Muslim friend who is a student at Central College, or of our family doctor from Pakistan. We may visualize oil wells and the price of gasoline at the pump. Or we may recall the sight of the Taj Mahal in India, one of the seven wonders of the world, or the great mosque, the Dome of the Rock, on the very site of Herod's temple in Jerusalem. We may remember the elderly Muslim we once saw in Cairo, quietly counting the beads of his rosary and repeating the "ninety-nine Beautiful Names" of God. Or we may think of the primary Muslim word for God, which is *Allah*. Allah means the God, the Almighty One beside Whom there is no other, and is the word used for God in the Arabic translation of the Bible. We may think of Muslim reverence for Muhammad (570-632 C.E.), whom Muslims respect more than any other human being, God's final and greatest prophet, the true example for human living. We may consider the Qur'an (sometimes spelled Koran), a book revealed through Muhammad. The Qur'an is about the size of the New Testament. Muslims regard it as the very word of God and cherish it as God's ultimate act of grace. Or we may recall the film that we saw of the pilgrimage to Mecca with its incredible sight of hundreds of thousands of joy-intoxicated devotees surging around the Kaaba, the holy shrine in Mecca, the center of Muslim devotion.

We may also think of the immensity of Islam, the second largest religion in the world. One out of every six people in the world is Muslim, and the population of Islam will increase by about 50 percent in the next twelve years.[11] At least forty-six nations of the world have a Muslim majority population. We may reflect upon the geopolitical importance of Islam. Since the second World War Muslim nations have emerged from their centuries-long depression and have become politically free, economically powerful, and psychologically buoyant. They represent a mighty force that affects every human being in the world. We may consider Islam in terms of its religious complexity. Muslims themselves think of their religion as simple, based on the short creed: "There is no god but God, and Muhammad is the Apostle of God." But this simple and straightforward confession is elaborated into a larger set of beliefs and practices, a huge construct of religious law. Within Islam there are also formal divisions such as *Sunni, Shi'a, Ismaili;* it is finally characterized by a broad range of opinion and differing points of view on almost every imaginable subject. Or we may think of the dynamism of Islam, an increasingly confident people with a mission to bring the world to God and to place all of life under the direction of God. Islam calls its own adherents, and the whole world, to surrender to God!

With these words, "surrender to God," we have come to the trunk of the Muslim tree. The central theme of the vast Muslim religion is summed up in the word "surrender." Sometimes the name of a religion does not tell you very much about its content. The situation is otherwise with Islam. The words *islam* and *muslim* reveal the core of the faith. In the past many Christians called Islam "Muhammadanism" and Muslims "Muhammadans." Muslims resent and reject these terms. A Muslim friend might very well say to you: "We do not like to be called

Muhammadans. Muhammadan implies the worship of Muhammad. You should be called Christian because you worship Christ. But we do not worship Muhammad. He is certainly the greatest man who ever lived, but we do not worship a man. We worship God. So please call us Muslims."

The word islam means "the surrendering," and the word muslim means "one who surrenders." The Qur'an (3, 19) declares: "Religion with God is surrendering." To whom am I to surrender? To God alone. What should I surrender? My whole life, my personal life and my life in society. How should I surrender? By obeying the commands of God revealed in God's Word and exhibited in the life pattern of Muhammad. What will my surrendering yield? It will give me the true perspective for life in this world, and a possibility of future happiness in heaven according to God's will.

It is the reality of God that "compels" the surrendering. If the word surrender is inscribed on one side of the coin of Muslim faith, on the other is the confession of Islam: "There is no deity other than God, and Muhammad is the messenger of God." Usually this confession is spoken in its Arabic form, *la laha illa lah, wa muhammadu rasul lahi.* The confession could be rephrased as follows: "Surrender to God, the only God, as revealed through His messenger Muhammad." The Muslim sense of God is well-nigh overwhelming. In the psalm-like words of the Qur'an, which all Muslims regard as the source of their faith:

> God
> there is no god but He,
> the Living, the Everlasting.
> Slumber seizes Him not, neither sleep;
> to Him belongs
> All that is in the heavens and the earth.
> Who is there that shall intercede with Him
> save by His leave?
> He knows what lies before them
> and what is after them,
> And they comprehend not anything
> of His knowledge
> save such as He wills.

> His throne comprises the heavens and the earth;
> the preserving of them oppresses Him not;
> He is the All-High, the All-glorious!
> (Qur'an 2:255)[12]

Islam emphasizes both the power of God and the unity of God. As the aspects of the divine power, God is the Creator, the Ruler and the Judge, the Sovereign of individual life and the Sovereign of the universe. It is appropriate for the forehead to touch the ground in reverence and awe before the One Who is Almighty Power. God's unity is equally important. To surrender means to recognize that there is no other being in the category of God. Life is not to be surrendered to anything else. The greatest sin in Islam is to raise any other being or any thing to the level and stature of God. God, however, is not only single but also singular; that is, God is the Transcendent One who cannot be compared to anything. There is therefore a hiddenness to God, and a distance from anything human, that goes together with the divine power and unity.

Yet, at the same time, God is also near to us. In a passage much loved by Muslim mystics, the Sufis, the Qur'an says (50, 15): "We [God] indeed created man; and we know what his soul whispers within him, and We are nearer to him than the jugular vein."[13]

Both in majesty and in nearness, God is to be worshiped for God's own sake and for no ulterior purpose. Thus, the noted female saint of Islam, Rabi'a, prayed this celebrated prayer:

> O God! if I worship Thee in fear of Hell, burn me in Hell; and if I worship Thee in hope of Paradise, exclude me from Paradise; but if I worship Thee for Thine own sake, withhold not Thine everlasting Beauty.[14]

While this inner aspect of Islam is virtually identical with faith, the surrendering also has an external aspect, and that is related to obedience. God, who is the Master, is also the Guide. God makes known the divine will to humanity, whose duty and glory is to obey. The surrendering is not only the surrendering of the heart in faith, but the surrendering of the will in life. For Muslims, therefore, the relation between God and humanity has a great deal to do with obedience (*ibadat*). The parallel term is servant (*abd*). The highest aspiration of a Muslim man or woman is to be regarded as a true and obedient servant of God. Another Muslim saint declared: "Enough of splendour for me to be Thy slave. Enough of glory for me that thou art my Lord. My God I have found Thee the God that I desire, make me then to be the creature that Thou desirest."[15]

Not only the individual but also society must be the servant of God. North Americans tend to be perplexed by the phenomenon of nations like Iran and Saudi Arabia, and to a lesser extent other Muslim nations where the laws of religion are the law of the land. The answer lies in the surrendering. All of life is to be surrendered to God. Politics and economics must bow to God, family and civil law belong to God. After all, as the first verse of the Qur'an declares, God is "the Lord of the Worlds." There is nothing outside the domain of God's sovereign will. This principle is expressed in the *shari'a*, the code of Islamic law, which covers the whole range of human life and guides Muslims in their daily conduct. If there is doubt as to how to live or what to do, it is sufficient for Muslims to consider the example of the Prophet Muhammad himself, whom God has made a "noble pattern for believers." Muhammad represents authentic humanity for our time as well as his. The voice of God calls Muslims to uncompromising obedience: "Then We set thee upon an open way (*shari'a*) of the Command; therefore follow it!" (45, 18).

The idea of surrendering runs like a thread that ties together the five basic beliefs and five basic practices of Islam. The beliefs include the following.

- God: To express their surrendering, Muslims constantly use phrases like "Glory be to God," "God is great," "Praise to God," and "if God wills," in their daily speech.
- Angels: From Gabriel, the angel of revelation, to Israfil, who will sound the last trumpet, angels view themselves as "the servants of the Merciful One" (43, 16).
- Prophets: From Adam, the first prophet, through Abraham, Moses, David, Jesus, and Muhammad, God raised up a stream of prophets to proclaim one basic message, *islam*, surrender, the natural, true universal religion of all humanity.

- Books: Through sacred books, including the Torah, Zabur (psalms), Injil (Gospel), the Qur'an, God reveals the divine will to which the servants of God should submit.
- Resurrection and Day of Judgment: Although the way of salvation in Islam is not finally defined, it is the Muslims, those who have surrendered, who may hope to enter "the abode of peace."
- Predestination: Although an increasing number of modern Muslims reject this notion, traditional Islam has added predestination as a sixth belief, underlining submission and resignation as aspects of the surrendering.

The basic practices of Islam similarly reflect the central theme of surrendering:

- Confession: That which officially makes one a member of the surrendering community is to declare that "there is no deity except God and Muhammad is the messenger of God."
- Prayer: Five times a day, Muslims humble themselves physically and spiritually in the liturgical drama of the Muslim prayer.
- Fasting: One month of the year (Ramadan), during the daylight hours, no food or water passes the lips, in order that believers may be trained in the art of surrendering.
- Charitable giving: A portion of the believers' goods must be surrendered to God for alms-giving to the poor. The amount varies, but is ordinarily 2.5 percent of the cash income above basic needs.
- Pilgrimage (*hajj*): The dream of every Muslim is that once in a lifetime he or she may join the company of pilgrims that make their way to sacred Mecca, where the call to surrender was given by the Prophet, as they cry out: "*Labbaika!*—I am ready for you, God!"
- Striving for God: Some Muslims add *jihad*, a term that means "to strive," as a sixth obligatory practice. The greater *jihad* is to struggle against the evil of your own soul, and the lesser *jihad* is to strive for God's victory in the wider world.

Salaam aleikum! That is the greeting which Muslims give each other when they meet. It means "peace be with you." The response that is given is *wa aleikum salaam!*, which means "and to you, peace." That is, "may you also have peace that comes from surrendering to God."

The core intuition of surrender that characterizes Islam and Muslims raises two questions for Christians: "What is the Christian idea of surrendering?" and "What is the good news in the gospel for Muslims?"

HINDUISM

It is now very easy to rent the film *Gandhi* at the video stores on First Street in Mainville. For a time there was a major rush on the film. The figure of the small man with glasses who changed the history of our century filled almost every screen in the town. The citizens of Mainville watched in fascination as the "Mahatma" ("Great Soul") rallied the people of India in a peaceful bid for freedom. Gandhi talked of nonviolence, of truth as love, of means as ends in the making. He cherished the hymn "When I Survey the Wondrous Cross;" a Christian missionary, C. F. Andrews, appeared frequently at his side. Yet Gandhi was clearly a Hindu. With sorrow, viewers watched as his life moved to a fateful conclusion. Even as, in the wake of the frenzies that marked the partition of India, he struggled for Hindu-Muslim understanding, he was assassinated by a right-wing Hindu. Although it was clear to viewers that Hinduism and India go together, nevertheless at that moment Delhi and Mainville seemed near to each other.

It is true that Hinduism has its home in India, but ideas and movements often leave home. So also, aspects of that religious complex called Hinduism have come to Mainville. Without being aware of the religious significance of their activities, a number of church members have joined Yoga and transcendental meditation clubs. At Central College, the Hare Krishna movement has become very active, and not a few parents are wondering what to say to their children who have been attracted by Krishna devotion. At the Mainville Library the Vedanta Society representative continues his series of lectures on a spiritual philosophy called monism (*advaita*). A casual reader picks up a copy of a recent *Atlantic* and reads Phoebe-Lou Adams's comment on a John Updike character. It is said that she is "that currently fashionable heroine, the middle-aged matron who flees luxury and a boring husband to find freedom, or her true self or, in Sara's case, spiritual enlightenment at an ashram somewhere in Arizona. Liberation from the gross material world is what she has in mind. . . ."[16] Ashrams in Arizona! At the same time, there are Hindu staff at Mainville's Memorial Hospital who display no visible outward religious marks or practices. Hinduism has arrived in Mainville, but what is it?

When we think of Hinduism, we may think of many things. We may think of the cow, sacred because it symbolizes life, and life is God. We may think of the Ganges River, where masses of pilgrims come to bathe in the holy waters. In their daily ritual bath individual Hindus recall the saving power of the goddess Ganga. We may think of the Scriptures of Hindus such as the Vedas and many others including the Bhagavad Gita, the "Song of God," the "book" of millions of Hindus today. We may also think of the caste system, which divides society along kinship lines; the sound of "*Ram! Ram!*" in home devotions, for since there is power in the Name of God, it is recited endlessly; the great religious festivals, when the deity is taken in triumphant procession on great stone vehicles pulled by thousands of devotees; the *sadhus* and *sanyasis*, the spiritually fulfilled persons who have "realized" God," and who spend their time in quiet devotion or as wandering mendicants. Or we may consider the practical Hindus of everyday life, a vast company of ordinary people busily involved in their tasks of making a living and rearing a family. They have a limited amount of time for religious practices, and some have only a modest interest in them. Yet beneath the surface of most Hindus runs a strong religious emotion, ready to spring forth at a moment's notice.

That emotion expresses itself in worship. Let us therefore in imagination proceed into a Hindu temple. But which temple? There is a bewildering variety of worship places, ranging from simple roadside shrines to majestic "cathedrals." This highlights a fundamental aspect of Hinduism: it is a family of religions.

Hinduism contains almost every possible religious belief and practice that could come to mind. Hindus view this great religious diversity as something that is natural and right, a proper expression of reality. Do not different human temperaments require differing religious approaches? The term "Hinduism," which implies that there is a unity of faith, was actually invented by Western scholars. Hindus themselves now accept the word as a useful collective noun, but it does not have the same meaning for them as "Judaism" and "Islam" do for Jews and Muslims.

Hindus would much rather glory in the fact that their religion has such variety and is ready to absorb and include new points of view. What binds the religion together is the faith that behind the Many is the One. The Rig Veda, the oldest Hindu Scripture, asks: "What is the One. . . . They call him Indra, Varuna, Agni. . . . The one Reality, the learned speak of in many ways."[17]

Although Hindus agree that there are many roads to the One Truth, some common patterns have developed. Worship is one example. Worship begins in the home, and fixed times and liturgical precision are important. At sunrise, every devout Hindu utters the "*Gayatri*," the most important of all Vedic verses (mantras), bowing toward the sun, the source of life:

> We meditate upon that adorable effulgence of the resplendent vivifier, *Savitar.* May he stimulate our intellects![18]

Hindus also worship in their chosen temples, although there is no set time for individual temple worship. At times the temple is relatively unattended; on other occasions it is very busy as individuals and groups conduct their devotions (*puja*). On festival occasions, which occur frequently, hundreds of thousands of devotees throng to the temples, caught up in an emotional frenzy of adoration and joy.

We usually think of Hindu temples as ancient structures, reflecting the fact that the religion of Hinduism goes back thousands of years. However, new temples are also being built in many places in the world. While not all of these are open to visitors, one of these, the great Birla temple in Delhi, with its curved, red-brick, myriad-towered magnificence, invites all to enter freely.

The Birla temple is somewhat different from many others. Most Hindu temples are dedicated to a single deity. The idol, which for some worshipers *is* God, for other worshipers *represents* God, is located in what is called "the inner sanctum," or holy place. The shrine is surmounted by a high tower and surrounded by a series of courtyards. Within the central shrine, the Brahmin priests take care of the idol, following a fixed daily schedule, dealing with it as if it were a living human being. The Birla temple, however, is deliberately composite. It is dedicated to all gods, thereby reflecting the basic spirit of Hinduism. As the worshiper enters, sandals are left at the door as a mark of respect. Flowers and incense are available in abundance, at a small price, to serve as offerings. Further in are the familiar figures of the faith—Siva, Vishnu, Krishna, Rama, Sita, Ganesh, Lakshmi. There are even memorials to Christ and Muhammad! The devotee selects a preferred shrine, presses the palms of the hands together and bows in reverence, offers words of silent prayer, presents gifts, and quietly withdraws.

> O gods! All your names (and forms) are to be revered, saluted and adored; all of you who have sprung from heaven and earth, listen here to my invocation.[19]

There is a sacred tree in India called the banyan. It is not the tallest, but it is the widest spreading tree in the world. The reason is that the roots drop from the branches and become like trunks of trees in their own right. Thus a single banyan becomes a kind of forest in itself. It takes a little effort to walk through and see the central trunk. Hinduism is a banyan tree. It takes special effort to identify its central theme. Some observers even say that it really has none, and to suggest that there is one is to miss the whole point of Hinduism. For them, Hinduism cannot be defined by any common core.

While there is some legitimacy to this point of view, it is also possible to affirm that there is in fact a trunk to the tree, and a central theme does exist. For there is one common desire that marks all Hindus: the desire to be freed from the bondage of this world, to be delivered from evil, and to become one with the Eternal. In fact, the core intuition of Hinduism may well be summed up by single words like "liberation" or "emancipation," or by the simple phrase "escape to the real." Hindus desire to escape from this world, to obtain spiritual release from the uncertainties and sorrows, the confinements and unrealities of this life, and to experience peace and eternal tranquillity. This fundamental emotion is well summed up in the famous Hindu prayer: "From evil lead me to good; from darkness, lead me to light; from death, lead me to immortality."[20] The whole point of the religious life ultimately is to escape, to escape to the real.

We are all familiar with the common exclamation, "That's for real!" Hindus want to get at the "that." What is it that is real? For Hindus, reality cannot be and is not to be looked for in this world and our life in it. All that we experience is provisional and is, ultimately, a form of illusion (*maya*). What seems to us to be real—this world, our life—is a shadow, as true as any shadow but not reality itself. Yet we are unfortunately in bondage to this world and our life in it. We live, as it were, in the shadows, and this accounts for all our grief. We must move out of the shadows into the sunlight of a greater truth.

There is another reality, the real Reality. We may understand it as the essential spirit of the universe that lies behind all the material things of this life. What is it called? Hindus give it different names: the One behind the many; *brahman*, the basis of the universe; *atman*, the world soul that permeates the universe. Where do you find this real Reality? Various Hindus give different answers to this question. Many of the greatest thinkers of the religion say: You find it within yourself! Brahman, Atman, the Real is actually your true and essential self. You have an outer self and an inner self. What you usually call "self" or the "ego" is your outer self, a surface, material thing. There is more to you than you think. Deep within you is your true self, and at that essential level your soul and the divine soul are one! Discover that, and you will be free.

Hindus do not hesitate to say that at this final level of reality, "humanity is God." This truth is expressed by the famous Hindu text: "Thou art That!" The relation of your soul to the world soul is that of a drop of water to the ocean. Essentially, both are the same. Not only that, but as the drop of water longs to return to its source and merge with the ocean, so also your essential soul longs for release. Human beings must therefore do two things. First of all, they must become aware of the wonder of their true being. Secondly, they must foster their personal escape to the real. When we do come to the realization of our essential unity with the eternal Brahman, characterized by existence, consciousness, and bliss, then we shall experience true existence, bondage-overcoming awareness, and eternal bliss. We shall have emerged from the shadows into the sunlight!

Such escape to reality does not come easy for human beings, however, for we are deeply locked into life in this world. What locks us in is a spiritual law called karma. Karma is the order of cause and effect, or the law of justice. This law declares that every action of a human being has certain inevitable results. These effects must be fully worked out if the law is to be satisfied and justice done. This law imprisons us in this world. Let us take an example. Suppose a dying person makes a will that produces great dissension among the heirs. That dissension, in turn, results in hatred that may continue for generations. That hatred again produces other effects that must be worked out. Like a stone in the water, a single human life through its actions, both good and bad, sets in motion waves upon waves of results, and by the inexorable law of karma, it is the setter-in-motion who must bear the full responsibility of those deeds and their effects.

The problem is not yet fully stated. It is clear that one life is not enough for all the results to be worked out and for the wheel of justice to run fully. Therefore, the human soul must be reborn into this world, again and again. So, joined to the doctrines of self and karma is a third teaching, the doctrine of reincarnation (samsara). After death, the essential human soul is reincarnated into this world in whatever form it deserves in the light of previous actions. So life in this misery-ridden world goes on, and on, and on. Hindus say that in the laws of karma and samsara we find the explanation for all the sufferings and inequalities of human existence. How, then, shall a person escape from this "passage of the inner soul through thousands and ten thousands of wombs," be liberated from this endless cycle, and escape to the real?

Hindus hold that there are many ways to liberation(*moksha*), since human beings vary. There is a way that is suited to every human level. The choice of the path depends on the stage the individual soul has reached on its pilgrimage to truth. Some people are at the earliest stage of their religious development, and for them a sacred tree or idol serves to satisfy their spiritual needs. Others may require communion with a personal god. Still others are at the stage where they think of God in philosophical terms.

This Hindu idea that there is an appropriate religion for each stage is called the principle of "spiritual competence." An associated principle is called "choosing your own deity." All believers have the perfect right to choose that deity and select that form of religion which helps them, at the same time refraining from passing judgment on the choices others make. Within this general framework, however, Hinduism teaches that there are three major paths to liberation. They are the way of knowledge (*jnana-yoga*), the way of devotion (*bhakti-yoga*), and the way of works (*karma-yoga*).

We have already touched upon the way of knowledge. According to this path one is liberated by becoming aware of one's identity with the divine spirit. At this point it will be useful to clarify the Hindu use of the term "yoga." First of all, yoga is used to describe the major path to liberation through knowledge. Secondly, yoga refers to a patterned system of physical-mental control that is applicable to all three paths to truth. Finally, it is also used to describe four subdisciplines (*mantra*, *laya*, *hatha*, and *raja* yoga) of the general practice of yoga, each of which have their special emphasis. These subdisciplines are used as spiritual methods by their practitioners.

The general practice of yoga is a physical-mental discipline carried on by many Hindus for their spiritual development. It is particularly cherished by those who follow the path of wisdom. Beginning with breath-control and following eight steps, the art of concentrated meditation yields mystical control and power. It enables one to remain in the posture of meditation for a long time and fixes the senses and mind on Ultimate Reality, until one finally realizes *samadhi*, oneness with the super-consciousness. The Law of *Manu* describes this intense spiritual method: "Delighting in what refers to the Soul, sitting in the postures prescribed by the Yoga, independent of external help, entirely abstaining from sensual enjoyments, with himself for his only companion, he shall live in this world, desiring the bliss of final liberation."[21]

The second option for those who seek escape is the way of loving devotion. It is closely linked with respect for the gods. For philosophic Hindus following the way of knowledge, the gods represent only a kind of preliminary truth that will be bypassed when Ultimate Reality is experienced. For most Hindus, however, the gods represent that Ultimate Reality in personalized forms. The gods are real, and my god is especially real for me! The deities are fervently adored. They respond to adoration by giving their devotees the grace to escape the evil of life and to draw near to them, becoming one with them in a loving union rather than in identity. The general name for the personal god is Isvara, which means "the Lord," but in poetry and praise the term, "the Beloved," is often used. Kabir (1440-1518 C.E.) sang that Name:

> This day is dear to me above all other days, for today the Beloved Lord is a guest in my house . . . My longings sing His Name, and they are become lost in His great beauty: I was His feet, and I look upon His Face and all that I have . . . My love has touched Him; my heart is longing for the Name which is Truth.[22]

The major Hindu deities are Siva and Vishnu. Siva represents the elements of both creation and destruction. Siva's power and energy is worshiped as the Feminine Goddess (*sakti*), under many names. Vishnu, on the other hand, represents the element of hope. From time to time, when trouble arises in the world, Vishnu becomes incarnate to save humanity, taking on such forms as Rama, Krishna, and even Buddha. As Lord Krishna, he offers this consolation to his followers: "Fix your mind on me, be devoted to me . . . So shalt thou come to me, I promise thee truly, for thou art dear to me" (*Gita* 18).[23] As the Bhagavad Gita steadily increases in importance in Hindu devotion, so also the worship of Krishna is becoming ever more popular. At the same time, new forms of Hindu piety keep on emerging and attracting followers from Bangalore to Mainville.

The third major path to liberation is the way of works. That means faithfully carrying out one's religious and moral duties, but without concern for results. By a spirit of detachment the karmic effects of human actions will be overcome, and release will be obtained. These actions are summed up in the concept of dharma, which means law and virtue and includes a broad range of religious requirements:

- Purification rites: These are essential to prepare one for life that will produce liberation.
- Caste duties: Every human is born into a certain caste, a role determined by the law of karma. Caste is therefore sacred, and every effort is made to preserve it through controlled marriage practices. An individual's caste serves the caste member as an extended family and as a kind of life support system. By the proper performance of caste duties, one may rise on the scale of caste in the next reincarnation. Despite modern criticism, caste remains as a powerful element of dharma.
- Life goals: An individual may have four life goals: pleasure, material success, moral living, and liberation. All are valid, but the greatest of these is liberation.
- Stages of life: Ideally an individual passes through four life stages: student, family person, one who withdraws for spiritual reflection, perhaps to an ashram (retreat center), and one who has attained the liberated state. This life structure is symbolic and is largely ignored in actual life today. It affirms the final goal: escape to reality.

At the heart of the Hindu dharma is the principle of nonviolence, ahimsa. The ethic of Hinduism is based on this principle. Ahimsa is the recognition that the eternal soul is present in all of life, and therefore all living beings, whether human, animal, or plant, are to be respected. It was Mahatma Gandhi who inspired many contemporary Hindus to interpret ahimsa not only as nonviolence but as positive love. This, he said, is the real meaning of the way of works. He called it "truth in life," that is, liberation to reality achieved through disinterested service and through works of love, not escaping this world but transforming it: "I can say with assurance . . . that a perfect vision of Truth can only follow a complete realization of Ahimsa. To see the universal and all-pervading Spirit of Truth face to face one must be able to love the meanest of creatures as oneself."[24]

Whether they express their hopes in somewhat simple terms or in complex philosophies, whether they ask *Devi*, "the Protecting Goddess," to deliver them from smallpox or discuss the nature of the Impersonal Absolute, in one way or another all Hindus seek liberation. For those who have experienced it at the spiritual level, who have come in touch with Reality, in the form of their Deity or in the form of *brahman*, the experience is described as an ineffable one that produces a sense of freedom and peace. The feeling is summed up by Tukaram (1598-1659 C.E.), a saint from the area of Maharashtra, who sang this song:

> I saw my death with my own eyes. Incomparably glorious was the occasion. The whole universe was filled with joy. I became everything and enjoyed everything. I had hitherto clung to only one place, being pent up in egoism (in this body). By my deliverance from it, I am enjoying the harvest of bliss. Death and birth are no more. I am free from the littleness of "me" and "mine." God has given me a place to live, and I am proclaiming him to the (whole) world.[25]

The sense of escape that characterizes Hinduism raises two questions for Christians: "What is the Christian idea of emancipation and reality?" and "What is the good news in the gospel for Hindus?"

BUDDHISM

In 1956, at the Sixth Council of Buddhism, held in Burma, Buddhists celebrated the two thousand, five hundredth anniversary of their founder's birth. At that time, they reaffirmed their faith and laid plans to communicate it effectively to the world. Long before 1956, however, Buddhism has been a world religion, and it is now a living presence in Mainville, USA. E. M. Layman reports the testimony of a midwestern American youth who adopted Buddhism as her faith:

> Julie, a university sophomore, described herself as one who, a year before, had been "filled with paranoid hate." She had believed that her home situation was intolerable, that nobody understood her, that everyone treated her unfairly. And she had believed that she couldn't do anything about her life other than to complain and express resentment, so she was depressed all the time. Then a boyfriend, attending the University of Illinois, had told her about Nichiren Shoshu [a Japanese form of Buddhism]. He kept urging her to try chanting, insisting that it

worked. But she was suspicious of anything she didn't understand . . . Her friend didn't give up, so she finally committed herself. She felt that there had been a real "human revolution" in herself, and said that for the first time she knew the meaning of social responsibility. Now she felt happy and fulfilled, and life was really worth living.[26]

Buddhism is present among us, and the Julies of America are symbols of its presence. But what does it represent? When we think of Buddhism, we may think of many things. We may think of mellow bells and incense, and the sound of chanting, the great temples of Bangkok and Rangoon, or countless statues of the Buddha, either cross-legged or recumbent in form but always bearing the half-smile of enlightenment. We may think of head-shaved monks in saffron robes, with their downcast eyes and ever-present begging-baskets or bowls. Or we may recall the benevolent face of the Dalai Lama, the Tibetan "Living Buddha," beaming at us from the cover of a national magazine. We may remember Buddhism's silent meditation, the Japanese tea ceremony, a painting conveying emptiness or infinity, or a quiet garden in Kyoto with a single rock and tree. Or we may remember words like Zen and nirvana. We may recall the classic teachings of Buddhism, its Scriptures with its two main divisions, *Theravada* and *Mayayana*, and its universal creed: "I take refuge in the Buddha, the Law and the Order." We may know about the bewildering variety within North American Buddhism with its range of denominations, some based on ethnic origins, some doctrinally based. Or we may think of our personal Buddhist friend who teaches physics at Central College, and who originally came to Mainville from Hawaii. When we think of Buddhism, we may think of many things.

To draw nearer in our effort to understand Buddhist religion, let us in imagination enter a Buddhist temple. We have already noted that Buddhism offers a wide range of philosophies and many differing forms of worship. In North America, the majority of Buddhists represent a movement known as Shin Buddhism, and within Shin a submovement called *Jodo Shinshu*. The *Jodo Shinshu* "church" is likely to be some sort of rented building which may have been used for other purposes previously and is not architecturally unique. The interior, however, has been altered to a temple format. At one end of the room is a statue of Buddha known as the Buddha *Amida*, a term that conveys the idea of compassion, for the *Jodo Shinshu* church stresses salvation by the grace and assistance of the Buddha to his followers. Therefore, Buddha's visage conveys a picture of benevolence, befitting one who attained salvation, but instead of entering paradise took a vow to help others to reach the same goal. Two smaller statues may stand on either side of the Buddha *Amida*. The atmosphere within the temple is warm and friendly. A priest may be reading from the Scriptures (sutras), and he may also deliver a meditation. The highlight of the service is when the worshipers go forward, bowing several times, and repeat the phrase: "Hail, Amida Buddha!" This is the famed *nembutsu*, a shortened form of the Japanese phrase, *namu amida butsu*. A rosary, wrapped around the hand, is a sign of humble gratitude for the gift of salvation that, it is said, makes life "worth living."

But what is that aspect of life which makes it not worth living? And what is that salvation which turns it around? Buddhism deals with these fundamental questions. It is not in the variety of Buddhist forms and expressions, but in the answers to these questions that we find the basic theme of Buddhist faith. What makes life not worth living is the suffering and pain that it involves. What makes life worth living is the fact that there is a solution to suffering. These are the primary Buddhist affirmations. We may, therefore, suggest that the core intuition that runs through all of Buddhism is: the extinction of suffering. To understand that intuition one must first obtain a sense of the personal experience of Gautama Buddha, the founder of the religion of Buddhism.

Gautama Siddharta (566-486 B.C.E.) was a Hindu prince of North India. Only later in life did he receive the name "Buddha," which means "the Enlightened One." It is significant that he grew up as a Hindu in a Hindu environment. This explains the striking similarities between some aspects of Buddhism and Hinduism, just as Martin Luther's Roman Catholic background helps to explain the relationship between Lutheranism and Catholicism.

Legend says that Gautama grew up as a kind of spoiled playboy, whose doting father tried to prevent him from seeing anything of life's suffering. The inevitable took place, however. When the wealthy young courtier did witness human pain, the sight of it changed his life, as well as the history of the world.[27]

First, Gautama saw an old man, and he was thunderstruck. "Shame then on life, if everything decays!" Then he beheld a sick man, and the effect on him was the same."If health be as frail as the substance of a dream, who then can take delight in joy and pleasure?" Then he saw a dead man, and he was emotionally crushed by the sight. "Woe to life so soon ended! Would that sickness, age or death might be forever bound!"

By this contemplation, the prince was projected into what has always remained the primary Buddhist concern, the problem of human anguish.

Finally, Gautama saw a hermit, and that sight signalled to him the likely path to deliverance and called to him to follow it. It was the Hindu solution—to somehow escape from the material world and its bondage by the education of the soul through spiritual discipline, and by attaining true wisdom. "This shall be my refuge, and the refuge of others, and shall yield the fruit of life and immortality."

Resisting his natural inclinations, as well as all the pleas of family and friends, Gautama became a wandering ascetic. He engaged in the most severe austerities, in what Buddhists call "the great renunciation."

This traditional solution did not work for Gautama. The greater his efforts, the more hopeless seemed the human condition. All his rigorous struggles simply had the effect of keeping him in the strong grip of karma, and involved him in endless reincarnation to experience the inevitable results of his actions. He decided to give up what seemed to him to be a hopeless course of action. Instead, he plunged into deep personal meditation on the meaning of life and the problem of suffering.

The answer came to him suddenly, in a flashing moment of illumination, as he was sitting under a pipal tree (later called the *Bodh* tree, the tree of enlightenment). His vision of truth seemed stunningly clear. He immediately communicated this truth to his friends in a series of famous sermons much loved by Buddhists everywhere. The first sermon, spoken in the Deer Park in Benares, was on the subject: "Setting in Motion the Wheel of the Law." His second was on "The Non-Existence of the Soul." He became famous for his teaching and attracted a huge following. Flouting the normal distinctions of caste and class, he allowed people from all ranks of society to hear him. They were attracted not only by his subject material and his rhetorical power, but also by his practicality, his analytic insight, his broad attitudes, and above all his compassionate spirit. When Gautama died after forty years as a wandering teacher, his last public words were: "I exhort you saying: Decay is inherent in all component things. Work out your salvation with diligence."[28]

Those words were consistent with the views that Gautama Siddharta had set forth so effectively. For many Buddhist believers he is the greatest human of all time, the enlightened teacher and noble human example. For others, however, the figure of Gautama Buddha transcends a historical description. For some of these believers he is a compassionate Savior (bodhisattva), while for others the Buddha is the Eternal Principle of the universe (*tathagata*). Whatever the point of view may be regarding the nature of his person, all of his disciples accept the Buddha's straightforward analysis of the human predicament. He taught these basic principles:

- Suffering, pain, sorrow is the universal human problem. Everything, even joy itself, is touched and ultimately spoiled by suffering.
- The source of suffering is human desire, whether that be a craving for pleasure, for prosperity, for power, or for life itself.
- Desire not only produces suffering in this life, but it also keeps a human being imprisoned in the endless cycle of suffering.
- The solution to the problem of suffering, therefore, is the annihilation of desire, "letting it go, expelling it, separating oneself from it, giving it no room."

The Buddha then carried his analysis farther. What produces desire, he asked. To what is it related? He answered, it is fundamentally related to and issues from the idea of self. At last the true culprit is revealed! There would be no desire, if there would be no preoccupation with self. Logically, step by step, Gautama

Buddha had followed the trail from suffering to desire to self. What is to be done with the problem of self? The trail of logic ended with Buddha's final and most radical conclusion, namely, that there is no such thing as a permanent self! The idea of permanent self is the product of ignorance, and that delusion must be considered the final root of the problem of suffering.

Attack the problem at its roots! The elimination of that delusion is for Buddha the ultimate solution to the problem of suffering. You must realize that what we call "self" is nothing more than a bundle of five material things: body, feelings, perceptions, emotions, and acts of unconsciousness. This heap of things comes together according to the law of karma, and creates a certain illusion of individuality. But, said the Buddha, self is like a chariot that can be disassembled into its component parts, and nothing called "chariot" is left.

> Strictly speaking, the duration of the life of a living being is exceedingly brief, lasting only while a thought lasts. Just as a chariot wheel in rolling, rolls only at one point of the tire, and in resting rests only at one point, in exactly the same way, the life of a living being lasts only for the period of one thought. As soon as that thought has ceased, the living being is said to have ceased.[29]

In reality, to use another analogy, life is like a river, a constant movement and becoming, and there is no such thing as a persisting and ongoing individual ego. This is the truth that overcomes humanity's grief. Awareness of this truth is enlightenment. Awareness of this truth blows out self-related desire and, in turn, annihilates desire-related suffering. Such awareness is, in fact, nirvana, the "blowing-out," the cessation of suffering, the heavenly "emptiness" that is yet full of "unspeakable bliss."

Gautama Buddha also identified the way that would lead to this enlightenment. He called it the "Eightfold Path," which includes right understanding and right-mindedness; right speech, right action, and right livelihood; right efforts; right mindfulness and right concentration.

Basically, the Eightfold Path places all responsibility on the individual and calls for rigorous intellectual, moral, and meditational discipline. Such discipline naturally led to the development of an order of monks, which was and is governed by ten precepts. Lay Buddhists are required to follow only the first five of these, namely, abstaining from the destruction of life, from theft, and from unchastity, from deception, and the use of intoxicants. Obedience to these precepts produces the character that in the end will make possible the extinction of suffering. There is nothing about "God" in all this. Everything depends on individual effort.

As time passed other Buddhists took a different point of view. There was a feeling that ordinary human spiritual power is not strong enough to enable one to follow the arduous path of self-discipline and obtain enlightenment and peace. They came to the conclusion that external help is required. This feeling linked with another development. It did not take long after his death before Gautama Siddharta began to be regarded as more than human. By some he was elevated to the stature of the divine and was regarded as the Heavenly Helper whom people need. Did he not stay in the world after his own enlightenment, in order to aid others to overcome suffering? Will not the Compassionate One come to our assistance also? So the great teacher of wisdom became Lord Buddha, the Blessed and Exalted One, the Lord of Mercy and Savior, the Victor and Ruler.[30] He is the external Power Giver who will offer grace and assist devotees to extinguish suffering and to attain nirvana.

Thus was born the idea of a bodhisattva. A bodhisattva is a wise individual, destined for enlightenment, who is dedicated to the salvation of others and works with compassion for suffering beings. Such a one postpones the attainment of personal bliss in order to help others. There have been many such Buddhas in the past and there will be others in the future. This idea mingled with the veneration of gods and developed into a full and complex body of religious belief and practice. Vasubandhu, a Buddhist seer who lived ten centuries after Gautama Siddharta, summed up the belief regarding the bodhisattva:

> But why do the Bodhisattvas, once they have taken the vow to obtain Supreme Enlightenment, take such a long time to obtain it?
>
> Because the Supreme Enlightenment is very difficult to obtain; one needs a vast accumulation of knowledge and merit,

innumerable heroic deeds in the course of three immeasurable world cycles. One could understand that the Bodhisattva seeks for the Enlightenment, which is so difficult to obtain, if the Enlightenment were his only means of arriving at deliverance. But this is not the case. Why then do they undertake such infinite labor?

For the good of others, because they want to become capable of pulling others out of this great flood of suffering. But what personal benefit do they find in the benefit of others? The benefit of others is their own benefit, because they desire it.[31]

Against this background, it is possible to understand what links together the various movements within Buddhism. All in their own way address the same problem.

- Theravada Buddhism (Sri Lanka, Burma, Thailand) affirms that each person must follow Buddha's example to overcome suffering, each person working out salvation for himself/herself, through following the Eightfold Path. Theravada Buddhists believe that they have remained closest to the Founder's teaching.
- Zen Buddhism (Japan and China) holds that there is an essential "Buddha-nature" in every human being, which must be realized. Salvation is the awareness of this cosmic unity that surpasses all "I-ness" and suffering. The realization may come in a flashing moment, through meditation, through reflection on a flower, through a slap, by dialogue with a master, or by reflection on a strange riddle such as: "What sound does the clapping of one hand make?"
- Mahayana Buddhism (China, Korea, Japan) holds that there are many enlightened ones who, like Gautama Buddha, are divine beings who come to earth out of compassion for suffering humanity. Some are teachers, some hear prayers, some share their accumulated merit with their devotees, and some perform special deeds of mercy; but they are all one in their common intention to help humanity overcome its grief. Nirvana is not a mind-state, but a place of joy, the pure land of bliss.
- Lamaism (Tibet) relates the reality of suffering to the existence of demonic powers. The Buddhist clergy are called Lamas, who use a variety of religious practices to attract the blessing of benevolent powers and drive off evil ones. Monastic life is important. The Dalai ("ocean wide") Lama is loved by all and is viewed as the living incarnation of the Savior Buddha.

The worshipers in the Jodo Shinshu temple in Mainville have almost completed their service. Again and again, with deep devotion and passion, they have called upon the blessed name of Amida, "the beloved Lord of the Pure Land," confident that thereby their burdens will be lifted and they may obtain the assurance of the promised land. Now they listen with serenity and hope to the lofty words of the *White Lotus Ode* that describes the promised land:

> What words can picture the beauty and breadth
> Of that pure and glistening land?
> That land where blossoms ne'er wither from age,
> Where golden gates gleam like purest water . . .
> There ne'er was a country so brightened with gladness
> as the Land of the Pure far off to the West.
> There stands Amitabha with shining adornments,
> He makes all things ready for the Eternal Feast.
> He draws every burdened soul up from the depths
> And lifts them into his peaceful abode.
> And who indeed is it with grace in his tones,
> Who sends his smile out to the dwellings of the suffering . . .
> Yes, it is God Himself, who sits on the throne
> And, by His Law, redeems from all need.
> With gold-adorned arm, with crown of bright jewels,
> With power over sin, over grief, over death.
> None is like to our God in his greatness,
> And none can requite his compassion's great power![32]

The dominant theme of overcoming suffering that marks the religion of Buddhism raises two questions for Christians: "What is the Christian idea of the extinction of suffering?" and "What is the good news in the gospel for Buddhists?"

CONFUCIANISM

The new club has just opened its doors on the west side of Mainville. It is called the T'ai Chi Meditation Center. Quite a number of Mainville citizens have taken advantage of the courses offered by the center. Those who attend them tell of the interesting body exercises they do. They witness to their improvement in the art of meditation, and speak of "feeling the vital force." They use phrases like *yin and yang* and talk about the right balance that must be maintained between the contending forces of human nature. Perhaps without realizing it, these Mainville citizens have come into contact with a thirteenth-century form of Confucianism, which was popularized by a noted Chinese thinker named Chu Hsi. T'ai Chi is only a small part of the much larger religion of Confucianism. In its broader form Confucianism has been present in North American cities for decades, concentrated in their large Chinese communities. But now some Mainville citizens are encountering it for the first time through T'ai Chi. This, it is said, is "the right way to go."

When we think of Confucianism, we think of many things. Above all we think of China. China has been called "the land of three religions." This term refers to the triple streams of Taoism, Confucianism, and Buddhism that have flowed through China, sometimes side by side and sometimes intermingling. It is a useful term, but one that ignores other important elements in Chinese religious history, both at the beginning and at the end.

At the beginning is the early seedbed of Chinese religion. At the end is the current philosophy of Chinese Marxism. Marxism has passed through various phases since 1949, when Chairman Mao assumed control of the nation. In principle, it was opposed to all religion. In practice, it particularly opposed what it regarded as the "foreign" religions, such as Buddhism and Christianity. But Marxism in China reserved its greatest displeasure for the heritage of Confucianism, which it regarded as hopelessly feudalistic and a symbol of reactionary bourgeois culture. Now the world watches in astonishment as contemporary China begins to take new and more positive attitudes toward religion. Even Confucianism, which had always remained as the deeply embedded substratum of Chinese culture, is being studied once again by Chinese scholars.

What, then, is Confucianism? Like Hinduism, the term "Confucianism" is a Western term that is used to cover a broad stream of philosophic thought and religious practice. It does, however, have the merit of drawing our attention to the founding sage, Confucius (551-479 B.C.E.), for whom the religion is named and whose ideas provide its dominant themes. Confucius is the

English form of Kung Fu-Tzu, or "Master K'ung," who was born the son of a poor but noble family. He was raised by a devoted mother who ensured that he would receive a proper education as a scholar. His deep love for education and conviction of its great importance remained with him all his life. When his mother died, he mourned for her for three years, thereby demonstrating the love of family ties that has always been such a prominent mark of Confucianism.

Confucius became a teacher and remained one for thirty years. He was popular partly because he put forward his ideas in a clear, orderly and pointed way that people could appreciate. But he was also known for the fact that his teaching went beyond the familiar subjects of history, manners, poetry, music, government, and religion. He sought to give a deeper instruction in the moral dimension of life and tried to be an example of moral living for his students. Basically, he believed in the importance of both manners and morality, and his emphases had tremendous impact on the educational system of the nation.

Finally, however, Confucius decided that it was not enough only to teach. He felt that it was important "to get involved." This conviction was brought upon him by the corruption and decadence of the society in which he lived. It was a time of great confusion and disarray, and Confucius came to the conclusion that the principles for which he stood could be made effective only if he entered governmental life. It was not that he believed that morality could be legislated, but he was sure that it would become contagious if it were well represented among leaders. Believing that humans are naturally good, he felt that if goodness is visibly present among leaders, the latent natural morality of humanity will also emerge and become a practical reality in everyday society. The whole society would be infected with goodness by the example of its leaders!

Confucius sought and obtained a civil servant's post and after a time rose to high position. He attempted to make his principles known and effective. However, through no fault of his own—he had objected to the immorality of the court!—he lost his position. From the ages of fifty-five to sixty-seven he wandered about, vainly offering his services to dubious princes, gathering some disciples, and encountering a variety of hardships. At last his home prince relented and invited him to return. Confucius accepted and spent the remainder of his life as a kind of consultant sage, continuing the thinking, teaching, and writing that eventually made him the most respected of all humans for many people over the course of centuries.

From the thoughts of Confucius stems the complex religion of Confucianism. Can we identify its core intuition and understand what it implies?

Some people have suggested that Confucianism, at least as Confucius taught it, is not really a religion at all! What is the basis for such a view? As we have seen, the Sage was concerned to build a true humanity. It is true that later on he virtually became a god for many of his followers, but his own interest was primarily in improving society in this world. Thus he did not speak very much about God and the supernatural. He was aware of their reality but felt that discussions of those essentially mysterious subjects would detract from the main issue—duty to humanity.

Confucius had the deepest respect for tradition. While he is regarded as the founder of Confucianism, he did not think of himself as a religious or social innovator, but rather as a transmitter of the wisdom of the ancients. He wanted society to recover the proven wisdom of the past and to apply it to the conditions of the present. Many of the principles that he espoused, therefore, must have been understood by his contemporaries. What he did, however, was to take those familiar ideas and intensify or focus them in a fresh way.

One example of this focusing was the traditional Chinese concept of tao, a word that basically means road or way, that is, "the common road for people to walk on . . . the principle people should follow in their daily affairs and human relations."[33] Confucius focused the principle in terms of right action. He placed it within the frame of reference of his practical appeal to moral living and to providing a harmonious social order. His primary concern was establishing the ethical basis of concrete human daily affairs. "The Way is the way in which Confucius thought that individuals, states and the world should conduct themselves and be conducted."[34]

What a contrasting picture this is from the religion of Taoism, which developed alongside Confucianism! Let us table our discussion of Confucianism for a moment to consider the different view of life called Taoism. Near the time of Confucius another great thinker arose in China whose ideas gave birth to Taoism. His legendary name is Lao Tzu. The book attributed to him, *Tao Te Ching*, has had immense influence, and one authority states that "no other book except the Bible has been translated into English as often as Lao Tzu's."[35] His ideas became widespread, perhaps affected Confucius himself, and certainly influenced later Confucianism.

Lao Tzu also took up the idea of tao, but from a different perspective than Confucius. He virtually identified tao with nature and came to the conclusion that the best way to express human life is not through studied habits but through natural behavior. Irving Berlin's song "Doin' What Comes Naturally" from *Annie Get Your Gun* might capture this idea.

Lao Tzu took his clue from nature. Look at the heaven and the earth, he said. They do not struggle in their course, but neither are they governed by a set of arbitrary laws and traditions. Rather, quietly and harmoniously, they yield themselves to the natural flow of events. Here, he pointed out, is the true pattern for living. It is not in structured educational training nor in organized human relationships that sages such as Confucius commended.

Lao Tzu taught that hidden within the natural flow of events is the mysterious tao, elusive, impalpable, indescribable, but very real. "Shadowy it is and dim; yet within it there is force."[36] It is the eternal order of things and the guiding force of the universe. According to Lao Tzu, wisdom is to be correctly attuned to the tao. To be correctly attuned to it, in turn, is to yield to it, to move with it, to live quietly, spontaneously, to merge one's life and being with the flow of nature, to be humbly compassionate, and to let life develop with individual freedom. When a Taoist was asked how to govern the world, he answered: "Let your mind find its enjoyment in pure simplicity; blend yourself into the ether in idle indifference; accord with the natural order of things; and admit no selfish consideration. Do this and the world will be well governed."[37] These ideas led to the philosophy and religion of Taoism. Through later Chinese history, Taoism changed and became a religion of mystical and magical power. It merged with superstitious forms of popular religion and largely lost its influence.

Since Confucius used homely analogies, it might be helpful to use word pictures to contrast him with Lao Tzu. You could think of Lao Tzu as a fisherman on a riverbank on a hot afternoon. With his hat pulled down over his eyes, he is contentedly holding a fishing pole in his hand. Confucius, on the other hand, you could picture as a college administrator, who both teaches industriously and, at the same time, is busy with his organizing tasks. A Taoist philosopher's imaginary story further illustrates the contrast between the two. In this tale, Lao Tzu asks Confucius to give him the gist of his message. "The gist of the matter," said Confucius, "is goodness and duty!" Lao Tzu responds: "Learn to guide your footsteps by Inner Power, and to follow the course the Way of Nature sets; and soon you will reach a goal when you will no longer need to go around laboriously advertising goodness and duty . . ."[38]

Obviously then, Confucius differed strongly from the approach of Lao Tzu. Goodness and duty for him were not "laborious" principles, but rather true reality! The harmony toward which humanity should aspire is above all a dynamic moral harmony. Thus he emphasized positive virtues such as human-heartedness, righteousness, loyalty, and altruism, as well as the inner disciplines of self-examination, patience, and restraint. Furthermore, he believed that wise moral living, both at the individual and social levels, requires cultivation. Behavior, therefore, should be carefully organized on the basis of these principles. Consequently, Confucius turned his energies to teaching and encouraging a life-style ordered in all its relationships. It would be based on sound moral training and reflect the moral harmony of the universe. Perhaps this life-style might be described as "practicing the art of sane living," but it involved something deeper than mere common sense. Behind these admonitions lay

Confucius's sense of the universally valid "Heavenly Mandate" making itself felt and being realized in human existence.

While later branches of Confucianism took different points of view on the various issues of the faith, all Confucians agree with the founding sage in his fundamental theme. What, then can we suggest as the core intuition of Confucianism? In its simplest form, it is: reverence for harmony. Stated in an expanded way, it is: sagely reverence for cosmic harmony, expressed in a moral human order.

The trunk of the Confucian tree is reverence for moral harmony, a deep respect for the right way to live as manifested in appropriate personal behavior and in cooperative human relationships. Confucius put the whole matter plainly when he said, "Harmony or moral order is the universal law of the world."[39]

We have already noted that Confucius himself did not really speak very much about "Heaven" (*tien*) or about the "High Ruler" (*shang-ti*). Both names are used for God. Although he said that the presence of unseen powers in the world is like the rush of many waters, he did not comment much about the realm of the spirits. In a sense Confucius was was very modern, reflecting a common attitude to be found among contemporary religious people of all kinds. One commentator declared:

> Here is the key, then, to Confucius' attitude toward religion. He believed in it apparently, but he was not much interested in it. It had to do with the realm of forces beyond man's control. But Confucius was interested in making over an intolerable world into a good world . . . He was occupied with the practical problem of how best to utilize such ability as we have to act effectively.[40]

At the same time, it must be remembered that the moral harmony that Confucians are called upon to reverence is one that is cosmic in dimension. It involves heaven as well as earth. What links heaven and earth in Confucianism is the principle of morality. Confucius once remarked: "To find the central clue to our moral being, which unites us to the universal order, that indeed is the highest attainment."[41] Therefore the moral duties of human life include: "promoting mutual confidence and social harmony," "strengthening the social ties and bonds of friendship," "worshipping the spirits," "feeding the living and sacrificing to the dead." All of these, Confucius said, represent "a great channel through which we follow the laws of heaven and direct to proper courses the expressions of the human heart."[42]

Confucius summed up this principle of morality in his form of the golden rule, "What you do not like yourself, do not do to others." He advocated the development of five cardinal virtues: kindness, righteousness, decorum or propriety, wisdom, and sincerity. He further called attention to five primary relationships on which society must be based, each of which are to reflect the dynamic application of moral principles. In summary, these are:

> kindness in the father, filial piety in the son; gentility in the eldest brother, humility and respect in the younger; righteous behaviour in the husband, obedience in the wife; humane consideration in the elders, deference in juniors; benevolence in rulers, loyalty in ministers and subjects.[43]

Against the background of *reverence for moral harmony* we view other important facets of Confucian doctrine and practice:

- *Yin* and *yang*: Within the universe and within each individual are two contending forces that some compare to the feminine and masculine respectively. These are "energy packs" which determine the flow of nature and human life. They must be balanced, controlled, and harmonious.
- *Li* in one form is natural law or reason. It is the rational principle underlying social discipline and harmony. *Li* in another form is the application of the principle in the form of worked out laws and rituals. Confucius summarized these ideas when he said: "Thus *li* must be based on Heaven, shows its actions on earth . . . (and) the duties of *li* are the main principles of life."[44]
- *Jen* is the moral sense in every human being, that which makes a person a true human and urges one forward to a genuine, morally ordered human life.
- *Ch'i* is the spiritual energy or vital force within the human being, as it were, the *tao* in you.

Perhaps the concepts of *li*, *jen*, and *ch'i* may be best understood by the analogies of law, conscience, and spirit.

Two additional elements of Confucianism deserve mention. The first is the model of the ideal human being, called *chun-tzu*, the sage or superior person. The goal to which individuals should aspire is to become wise, moral, and "gentlemanly" persons, harmonious within themselves and in relation to others. The *chun-tzu* is the perfectly adjusted individual of virtue and equilibrium, who expresses the *jen* within and follows the external guidance of *li*. That person has reverence for harmony and is on the right way.

The second element is respect for ancestors. It has already been noted that filial piety is a fundamental human virtue. In fact, it is of such importance that respect for parents and forebears should on no account end when they depart this life. Why should they be forgotten or neglected? Their spirits have not gone far away. Because they remain near enough in nature to be interdependent and real enough for communion, they should be remembered and venerated. Remembrance is expressed in various ways, including ceremonies and offerings, especially at the time of the New Year. By maintaining a respectful contact, particularly with the most recent ancestors, one maintains the principle of cosmic harmony.

After Confucius died, his disciples kept alive his memory and teaching. Their profound respect for him was well-expressed by Mencius, acknowledged to be his greatest disciple.[45] His thoughts were transmitted, debated, and promoted in various forms. During his lifetime Confucius had interpreted some of the classical Chinese writings, and after his death his followers gradually put out *The Four Books* (the most important of which is *The Analects*), which reproduced and developed his teachings. Still, many discussions and arguments revolved around precise teachings of the Master in regard to familiar questions such as, Is humanity innately good or evil? Should morality be promoted by example or legislated by law? As a result, different trends and schools of thought developed within the Confucian tradition. In addition, other religious movements were developing side by side with Confucianism. Eventually, however, Confucianism won out as the state religion in China and impressed its influence indelibly on the nation's life, molding its thought, its character, and its ideals.

The development of Confucianism took another turn when Confucius himself was elevated from the position of a great sage to that of a semi-divine or divine being. Temples began to be erected in his honor and quickly became numerous. Images of Confucius were placed within the temples, and worship was carried on in his name. The state formally validated these practices and great public ceremonies were conducted at set times of the year. Sacrifice to Confucius was declared to be equal to sacrifice to Heaven. Confucianism was now, without controversy, a religion!

At the popular and domestic level, the veneration of Confucius blended with traditional religious attitudes and practices, especially the recognition of gods, ancestors, and spirits. Earlier we mentioned the primitive seedbed of Chinese religion. It was marked by a sense that the land is alive with spirits. Chinese had sought from ancient times to appease the spirits, using a variety of priests, healers, shamans, diviners, and magicians. This heritage became a living part of Confucianism at the popular level. It was expressed through a variety of familiar religious objects and activities, including household gods, candles, incense sticks, offerings of food, festivals, flags, firecrackers, and vows. Beliefs and practices of both Buddhism and Taoism were drawn into the Confucian picture. Here is a description of a Confucian household shrine in the 1940s:

> The shrine is situated in the central portion of the second floor of the west wing of the home. It is installed on the ground floor only when the house is a one-story structure. Occasionally the shrine is for ancestors only, but more often it houses a number of popular gods. Ancestors are represented in such a shrine either on a large scroll or on separate tablets. The scroll is a large sheet of mounted paper containing names, sex, and titles of the ancestors who are (theoretically) within *wu fu*, or five degrees of mourning . . .
>
> The popular gods in all family shrines are three: Kuan Kung . . . (the warrior from three kingdoms), Confucius, and one or more Buddhas. A fourth popular figure is the Goddess of Mercy

> or Fertility (*kuan-yin*). As a rule these goddesses are represented by images. In addition, there are often other spiritual figures in family shrines which the family members cannot identify. In at least one shrine there was a large tablet for Confucius as well as his supposed image. Before the shrine is an offering table, on which there are two incense burners, one for ancestors and one for gods, two candlesticks, and a flower vase or two. At the foot of the table are two round straw cushions for the kneeling worshipper.[46]

From San Francisco to Singapore, from Vancouver to Beijing, countless Confucian believers today would probably feel at home with this description.

If Confucianism began as a form of religious humanism, it ended as a form of human religion. But despite a broadening of the river of Confucianism into a delta of religiosity, the figure of the steersman, the Sage, remained and remains a constant factor. All Confucians would echo the words of Mencius: "Wherever ships and carriages reach, wherever the sun and moon shine, wherever frosts and dews fall, all who have blood and breath unfeignedly love and honour him. Hence it is said: 'He is the equal of Heaven.' "[47] Confucius himself put it much more simply: "As to my being a sage and a true man, I am not so presumptuous: I will admit, however, that I have unceasingly tried to do my best and to teach other people."[48] The Confucian reverence for harmony raises two questions for Christians: "What is the Christian idea of harmony and moral order?" and "What is the good news in the gospel for Confucians?"

PRIMAL RELIGIONS IN NORTH AMERICA

Bear Creek Indian reservation is located a few miles west of the town of Mainville. Many Indians have moved permanently into the town. There they have joined the broad streams of Mainville life and are employed in various professions and occupations. Although they daily rub shoulders with their fellow citizens, few non-Indians have much real knowledge of how Indians view their history and life. Distorted images are still formed by memories of old Hollywood movies!

A majority of the Indians who work in Mainville have preferred to live on the reservation at Bear Creek. One of the reasons is that the Indian community there is very enterprising and progressive. It has used its resources with great wisdom. Schools, small businesses, restaurants, and recreational establishments dot the area.

In the middle of the reservation a splendidly constructed cultural center is often used by many Mainville groups who wish to conduct retreats in a natural setting. The architect of the whole development is Chief Adam Stonechild. A brilliant, highly educated, and determined leader, he is also an ordained minister in a major Christian denomination. When he addresses groups of visitors, which he is always ready to do, he conveys a great natural dignity and his words echo the deepest respect for his own cultural heritage. As his listeners quickly come to realize, that heritage includes his religious tradition. The face of the elder glows with inner emotion as he describes Indian spirituality.

What is that religious tradition which is fused with Adam Stonechild's Christian faith? What is the content of the Indian spirituality? Before we deal with these questions and also suggest the dominant theme of native Indian religions in North America we need to look at the larger context of primal religions.

Many regard native North American traditions as belonging to a wider religious stream called aboriginal or primal or traditional religions. Many other adjectives have been used from time to time to describe these religions with their millions of adherents in the world even today. In older writings, they are sometimes referred to as primitive or early religions. Primal religions are also referred to as animistic religions, that is, having to do with spirits. Other adjectives commonly used for these religions include: tribal, folk, indigenous, and native.

When we consider the primal religions of the world, we think of a vast, bewildering, and highly complex spectrum of religiosity. They range across many cultures and embody unique elements in their individual forms. From New Guinea to Wyoming, from Peru to Dahomey, from the Philippines to Italy, from Haiti to Siberia, primal religion is alive, but greatly diverse. Yet, despite this variation, it is possible to see some common elements in the total picture. Not all of these common factors are found everywhere or in the same proportion. However, taken together they reveal the general characteristics of what we are calling primal religions:

- All of existence is viewed as a whole, and human beings are essentially part of nature. Nature itself has a sacred quality and is to be revered. The special term "religion" is rarely used. Rather it is believed that there is a sacred quality to all of life. Thus the terms natural, sacred, and spiritual overlap in meaning.
- A human being consists of more than one part. Besides the body, there may be a soul or several souls (often called spirit, breath, or shadow) all of which are believed to have reality. Dreams, visions, and communion with the spirits are important.
- Extraordinary or "supernatural" powers are an unseen reality in the world and cause both attraction and trembling. The powers may be present in matter or become expressed in spirits. It is essential that humans relate correctly to them.
- The sacred powers are manifested both in the ordinary things of life and in more startling ways. Any aspect of organic life such as natural objects (trees, rocks, eagle feathers) or natural activities (eating, dreaming, making love) can in a sense become "sacramental." At the same time, particular individuals such as prophets, medicine men, shamans, and warriors may receive special powers.
- Stories, myths, symbols, and ceremonies provide clues to the fundamental questions of life. There is teaching, but little attention to formal doctrine. Answers to questions are more felt than conceptualized. The repetition of stories and ceremonies bring participants into sacred space and time.
- Sacred sound and the spoken word have a real potency; they can make things happen. This is one reason why the majority of primal religions depend on oral tradition rather than on written scriptures.
- Group-mindedness is strong. Tradition and custom are all-important. Religious rituals serve to support the institutions, customs, values, and goals of the group. Fellowship is expressed through the communal ceremonies. Individual choice is present, but its limits are understood and observed.
- Morality is strongly related to custom. It is not always directly related to religious or ethical ideas. Taboos are as important as positive commands, and sin consists in breaking them. Pollution is to be

avoided; and when it occurs, it must be purified. Life cycle events such as birth and death, as well as blood, have special danger.

- The need to appease and/or control the powers leads to the use of magic. There are many different kinds of magic.
- There is resistance to change, for old beliefs and practices are proven and safe. They are unifying, comfortable, and satisfying. In fact, they are in a sense sanctified, and to lose them means to become desacralized. Adaptation takes place, but it is not easy. Rapid change brings trauma.
- Above all, the orientation of primal religions is pragmatic. They give practical assistance so that people can survive and relate properly to reality. Their function is "to save," but with emphasis on this life. While life does not end with death, the future lies in a hazy mist.[49]

Examining factors such as these can help us identify the common theme that runs through all primal religions. The best way that can be done, however, is to consider actual religions themselves. Let us therefore turn to North American Indian[50] religions. While there may be as many individual Indian religions as there are Indian tribes, we may ask: Is there not a common voice that speaks to us? If so, what does it say?

Religion and culture cannot be separated in primal religions, and this is certainly true in native North American Indian traditions. The religious situation is intertwined with the total development of the Indian nations. To understand Indian religions today we must therefore place them in the context of general Indian emotion and concern. Three major interrelated developments, in particular, preoccupy Indians and, therefore, affect our understanding of living Indian religion. First, Indians are searching for and recovering their roots. Second, Indians are reappraising and reappropriating their original religious traditions. Third, Indians are appealing for justice, especially as that relates to the land.

We may deal rather quickly with the first development, namely, that North American Indians are seeking for and recovering their roots. The search for roots is a well-nigh universal drive. Whether a white German-American is trying to find out when his forefathers left Magdeburg and emigrated to the Ukraine, a Black American is searching for her tribe in West

Africa, or a Cree Indian is contacting an aged person to find out what the elder has been told, the fundamental drive is very similar. All are looking back with appreciation to their past.

Indians have always honored the past. For them the past is made present through story, song, and ritual. But now the appreciation of their heritage is being consciously emphasized in many different ways by Indian communities, and the task of recovering their roots is complicated by two factors. In the first place, a partial adaptation has already taken place with another culture, the dominant, and sometimes oppressive, white American culture. There is no simple way of turning back the clock. In the second place, the natural Indian culture is a holistic one; that is, it is like a tapestry with all the threads interwoven. The recovery of roots, therefore, also means that there must be some sort of repossession of the original religious heritage.

This takes us to the second development: A serious reappraisal and reappropriation of indigenous religious tradition is currently under way among North American natives. It must be understood that the vast majority (perhaps over 90 percent) of North American Indians are baptized Christians and are not, therefore, simply members of primal religious groups. This situation produces a series of delicate questions. What values can be affirmed in one's native, pre-Christian religious tradition? What does the reappraisal and reappropriation of that tradition imply? Is it a choice among total acceptance, total rejection, or some sort of partial acceptance/rejection? What does loyalty to the gospel require, and what freedom does it offer? It is clear that native North American Christians today are struggling with many of the same questions that have preoccupied, and still engage, new Christian believers from Hindu, Buddhist, Islamic, or other backgrounds. While such an engagement involves tension, the Christian experience is that it may also make for an alert and lively Christianity.

The struggle and questioning produces mixed reactions in the native community. For some there is perplexity, for others spiritual travail and fear for the faith. For still others the answer is to affirm the positive strengths of both traditions and to regard them as complementary in value. Allan Wolf Leg, a Blackfoot Indian, stated this third view:

> I myself was born in the Indian way of life, but I was put into another, the white way of life, and then came back. As a result, I am between two lives . . . In that faith, there is God, our God, Jesus Christ, and the white people. In the Indian religion, there is God, the Indian people, and Nature between. . . . So what did they call this?—Paganism! . . . Before white men came God had given us directions on how to pray, but we did not have a Church like white people. O.K., our Church was the land, the sky, the stars; our altar, the strongest object that God created, the sun. . . . Compare the crucifix and the sun—one is a reminder of sin and death, the forgiveness of sins, and the other is a giver of life, strength, growth, birth.[51]

And a friend of his, named Carl, added: "I would like to say that to me our religious ceremonies are more spiritual than the other. I am a Christian too. I am happy to be able to say that I have two religions."[52]

The third related development in Indian culture today is the cry for justice, especially as it is related to control of the land. This is not a new phenomenon. A century ago, fighting helplessly for the land that had been taken away from them, Kiowa Indians uttered a prayer for help to the Great Mystery of the universe:

> My father has much pity for us.
> My father has much pity for us.
> I hold out my hands toward him and cry.
> I hold out my hands toward him and cry.
> In my poverty, I hold out my hands toward him and cry.
> In my poverty, I hold out my hands toward him and cry![53]

This kind of appeal is not restricted to North American natives. All over the world, members of indigenous traditions reflect the same concern. None has stated the case more poignantly than Fred Wandmaker, who spoke for Australian aborigines. In his parable, "Aboriginal Traveller," he paraphrased the story of the good Samaritan:

An Aboriginal person was going down the
road from birth to death in Australia
He fell among some goodhearted people who
gave him
Grog
Sugar
Tobacco
the Gospel
and they took his land
They left him by the edge of
the town
the desert
the mining camp
disheartened. . . . dispossessed. . . . and
dying.[54]

Wandmaker's eloquent cry cannot be fully understood if it is simply viewed as an appeal for justice. The aboriginal concern runs deeper than the principle of fair dealing. It is rather a cry for the recovery of a sacred identity with nature and an end to the disorientation that accompanied its loss.

This hunger for the land, and the aboriginal prayer to the powers for help, brings us close to the core intuition of Indian religions.

The core intuition, we suggest, may be expressed as: resonating with the universe and its powers or sensing one's spiritual oneness with the sacred universe and relating successfully to its powers.

Four basic ideas are included within this theme of resonating with the universe and its powers. The number four is of special significance in Indian tradition. For example, the "four winds" and the "four directions" have great importance, illustrated by symbols like the Ojibwa wand. Similarly, we can speak of "four thoughts" in the core intuition that meet in a common center. They are:

- sensing one's kinship with nature in a sacred universe;
- being aware of the Great Mystery, in and beyond what is seen;
- dealing with its powers and the ever-present spiritual forces;
- living harmoniously with the sacred land.

The "first thought" is kinship with nature. Native North Americans view life from a mystical-spiritual perspective. They believe a spiritual unity binds all in the universe together. Everything may have its own outward form—rocks, trees, stars, plants, animals—but all these have soul and personality and power, just as humans do. Taken together, they all constitute one family. "Thus, the universe of the Indians was filled with spiritual entities, all of which claimed the Indians as their kin."[55] Kinship with nature is stressed in the various creation stories that abound in Indian mythology. Some stories may tell of humanity born out of the earth's dark underworld, while others describe human life coming from the heavens. Yet all these stories have a common element: the affirmation that human beings are closely related to the other aspects of creation.

The fact of such kinship places Indians on a very familiar basis with the elements of nature. Animal spirits have great prominence, and communication with animals abounds in Indian legend. One could—and should—apologize to the deer even when hunting it! Bear is the "grandfather/grandmother"and is especially revered among some tribes. As for Coyote, that trickster, watch him like a hawk! The fact that elements of nature have not only personality but also power breeds fear as well as familiarity. There is special awe before the great powers, the winds, the thunder, the mother earth, and the life-giving sun. It is also clear that there are other powers which for some reason are hostile, and these need to be dealt with in special ways.

Viewing life from the perspective of a sacred kinship with the universe creates a special attitude to the ordinary things of life. It means that nothing is really ordinary and mundane. Looking at an old cooking pot, Lame Deer spoke to a white friend:

> What do you see here, my friend? Just an ordinary old cooking pot, black with soot and full of dents . . . It doesn't have a message, that old pot, and I guess you don't give it a thought . . . But I'm an Indian. I think about ordinary, common things like this pot. The bubbling water comes from the rain cloud. It represents the sky. The fire comes from the sun which warms us all—men, animals, trees. The meat stands for the four-legged creatures, our animal brothers, who gave themselves so that we should live.

> The steam is living breath. It was water; now it goes up to the sky and becomes cloud again. These things are sacred. Looking at that pot full of good soup, I am thinking how, in this simple manner, *Wakan Tanka* takes care of me. We Sioux spent a lot of time thinking about everyday things, which in our mind are mixed up with the spiritual . . . We Indians live in a world of symbols and images where the spiritual and commonplace are one. . . . We try to understand them not with the head but with the heart, and we need no more than a hint to give us the meaning.[56]

The "second thought" refers to the awareness of the Great Mysterious. When Lame Deer used the term "*Wakan Tanka,*" he was referring to the Great Mysterious, which is in and beyond the universe. Observers have debated whether Indian religions have anything comparable to the concept of the Supreme Being. Some argue that terms such as *wakanta*, *orenda*, and *manitou*, which are sometimes translated as "Great Spirit," really refer to an impersonal power. They suggest that the Christian idea of God has been woven into these Indian concepts, and that the idea of a Supreme Being is not naturally there.[57] What can we say, however, about the moving song of the Pawnees?

> Tirawa, hearken! Mighty one
> Above us in blue, silent sky
> Behold! We in thy dwelling stand![58]

The famed Black Elk, native theologian of Indian religion, declared:

> We should understand well that all things are the works of the Great Spirit. We should know that He is within all things: the trees, the grasses, the rivers, the mountains, and the four-legged animals, and the winged peoples; and even more important, we should understand all this deeply in our hearts, then we will fear and love, and know the Great Spirit, and then we will act and live as He intends.[59]

It is clear that the animistic beliefs and veneration of natural powers that mark popular Indian religions are accompanied by the feeling of an ultimate power. There is a movement from lesser powers to greater powers, and a sense that behind them all is the chief of powers. "The ultimate source of all powers or forces in the universe, power that was single and yet divisible, like the radiation of the sun; power that was actually divided, not only among lesser deities, but among all the objects of nature, including man himself."[60]

The "third thought" deals with the powers. Wisdom and survival require a correct handling of the powers on a practical level. This need is a major factor in the development of the complex ritual and practice of North American Indian religions. The search for a meaningful relation with the powers is illustrated by the famous quest for a vision, that is present in many different forms in various tribal traditions. In this quest, a youth goes in search of a guardian spirit. He has long been prepared for the moment. With mingled fear and anticipation he retreats to a high and lonely place. He has taken nothing with him, except possibly an offering. He engages in a rigorous four-day fast, quiet except for the spontaneous prayer that marks Indian tradition. Almost naked, exposed to the elements, he carries on a private vigil, awaiting the revealing of his power. Awake or dreaming he trusts that some animal or bird will reveal itself to him in spirit. Out of that revelation he will obtain a share of the creature's power, some direction for life, a physical totem, and perhaps a private song. Above all, he will now have a personal guardian spirit with a special strength upon which he can draw in moments of greatest need.

The powers must not only be revered; they must be implored, used, and, as far as possible, controlled for successful living. This fact is illustrated by the tradition of the sweatbox. This is a small, specially constructed, sauna-like hut, where for four days a devotee engages in a kind of sacred steam bath. All the chief elements of the universe—rocks, water, fire, and steam—join together in the sweatbox to provide a physical and spiritual purification that enables one to relate positively to the powers. The medicine man, in his turn, harnesses the powers for healing, while the shaman or diviner is personally possessed by a spirit, enabling him to provide a resource for dealing with problem situations.

Families, clans, and tribes also seek to control the powers with private medicine bundles. These bundles contain ordinary objects such as pebbles, bird and animal skins, feathers, teeth, hair, tails, pigments, and other items; but they have become holy, containing living spirits with practical power. Opened with the greatest care and complex rituals, medicine bundles release their powers to ensure success in such endeavors as hunting, love, warfare, and healing.[61]

In the four-day sun dance of the Plains Indians, a kind of annual "thanksgiving" ceremony is conducted. At this great event, emotion-packed dancing takes place around a central pole, marking the unity of existence. Song and dance are accompanied by flagellation of the body, symbolizing that true response to the Mystery requires sacrifice and suffering. Above all, the sharing of the peace pipe unites many of the themes we have discussed. The sweet grass, the breath of the individual, and the rising smoke bring the forces of life into harmonious balance, reaffirming oneness with the Great Mysterious and the creation, causing those sitting in the sacred human circle or hoop to declare, "We are related!" As one Plains Indian said:

> This I confess is the experience of the pipe ceremony. One has the strong and inspiring sense that gathering into the sacred hoop are all the powers, all the creatures of the universe. All are there to witness your concern and to pray with you. It is the sacred hoop indeed that is created and in the hoop health and happiness are given to each worshipper and to the whole community of creatures, human and other-than-human.[62]

The "fourth thought" indicates that the traditional Indian believer seeks to maintain a harmonious relation with the land. Indians believe that they have a covenant with the land. This covenant requires them to recognize in land the presence of the sacred, to deal with land well, and to integrate their lives with it. The Indian land claims that occasionally make news headlines certainly have a great deal to do with practical economic considerations, ranging from trapping grounds to oil fields. But at the root of the concern is a spiritual dimension. As they called for the fulfillment of treaty obligations, Canadian Indian leaders met in July 1988 to draft resolutions on land claims, education entitlements, tax exemptions, and services for off-reserve Indians. The huge meeting took place on a sacred ceremonial ground at the Beardy Reserve in Saskatchewan. "It's going back to the traditional type of spiritual gatherings that we had prior to treaty signing," said Chief Irvin Starr of the Starblanket Reserve.[63] When Indians claim the land, they are really claiming their spiritual being and praying for its fulfillment.

It is this fourth-wind aspect of their tradition that Indian Christians are earnestly attempting to share with white Christians. They view themselves as specially privileged to be able to speak of the relatedness of all created things, and to contribute a spiritual insight that will provide freshness to a theology of creation and a truly Christian ecology. The following statement, drawn from a Conference on Native Ministry, was presented by Indians to a Lutheran church convention in 1986 as a resolution for adoption:

> That the Native people have a covenantrelationship with the Creator which teaches that the land is sacred and they have a responsibility to care for it. This relationship establishes the aboriginal rights to the land as well as the spirituality which supports native cultures.[64]

Not surprisingly, in view of the history of human relations in North America, the resolution could not be passed but was rather tabled to a committee for discussion! In Mainville today, white and Indian Christians walk side by side, one in faith, but with mind and spirit still barely touching.

Further along in Fred Wandmaker's "Aboriginal Traveller" noted earlier, the author describes how a severely injured Aborigine traveler was finally helped. After the church warden and parish priest pass by unheeding, "another Christian came that way. She got off her stereotype and out of her preconception. Sitting down she listened and heard the wounds and the treatment. She poured in the oil of identification and support."[65]

The desire to resonate with the sacred universe and its powers, expressed in Native North American traditions, as well as in other primal religions, raises three questions for Christians: "What is the Christian idea of the powers?" "What is the appropriate response to the Indian belief that we humans have kinship with nature and a covenant with the land?" and "What is the good kinship with nature and a covenant with the land?" and "What is the good news in the gospel for adherents of primal religions?"

SUMMARY

Risking oversimplification, we have been trying to identify the core or dominant intuition that marks each major religion that shares the world with Christianity:

- for Jews, it is "belonging to God"
- for Muslims, it is "surrender to God"
- for Hindus, it is "liberation to reality"
- for Buddhists, it is "extinction of suffering"
- for Confucians, it is "reverence for harmony and order"
- for Indians, it is "resonating with the universe and its power (or powers)."

The core intuition of Christianity—its own dominant theme and magnetic center which determines the attitude, life, and hope of Christians everywhere—is somehow tied to the name of Jesus the Christ who calls himself the Light of the World. Each one of the other key themes we have noted echoes a deep sense of need and a profound longing. Christians claim that Jesus Christ has a relation with all who share those needs and longings. To describe how that relation is to be understood is the task of the theology of the church. To explain how that relation is to be fulfilled is the task of the mission of the church. The theology of the church and the mission of the church work hand in hand to address these religious instincts of humanity in such a way that many people may be able to witness the glory of God in the face of Jesus Christ.

Notes

1. Definitions not otherwise documented are the author's own.
2. David B. Barrett, "Annual Statistical Tables in Global Mission," *International Bulletin of Missionary Research* 12.1, (January 1988): 17. The figure for Chinese religions, however, is from Barrett's *World Christian Encyclopaedia* (Nairobi: Oxford University Press, 1982), 6.
3. Ibid.
4. Wilfred Cantwell Smith has made this point in several of his publications. He has also argued that every individual religion is new every morning.

"Fundamentally one has to do not with religions but with religious persons." *The Meaning and End of Religion* (New York: Mentor, 1964), 138, et passim.

5. Quoted by J. M. Kitagawa, "The History of Religions in America," *The History of Religions: Essays in Methodology*, ed. M. Eliade and J. Kitagawa (Chicago: The University of Chicago Press, 1959), 23.
6. Joachim Wach, "The Meaning and Task of the History of Religions," in J. M. Kitagawa, ed., The *History of Religions* (Chicago: The University of Chicago Press, 1967), 11. I acknowledge that there are other ways of studying a religion. For instance, the most common way is to describe each of the various beliefs and practices, history and habits of a religion, in some detail, in the manner of books titled "Introduction to World Religions." This might be called the cable approach. Each religion is regarded as a thick rope made up of many individual strands, and each strand is examined and described. A second way of studying a religion is the problem-solution approach. What human problem does a religion visualize and profess to solve? What is its analysis of the human condition and the improvement that is needed, desired, and offered? This approach assumes that every religion, in one way or another, has to do with "salvation."
7. Jacob Neusner, *The Way of the Torah: An Introduction to Judaism* (Encino, Calif.: Dickenson Pub. Co., 1976), 127ff.
8. Abraham J. Heschel, *Man is Not Alone: A Philosophy of Religion* (New York: Farrar, Straus & Giroix, Inc., 1976), 127ff.
9. Louis J. Finklestein, "The Jewish Religion: Its Beliefs and Practices," in Finkelstein, ed., *The Jews: Their Religion and Culture* (New York: Schocken Books, 1971), 469.
10. Prayerbook Committee of the Rabbinical Assembly, ed., *Weekday Prayer Book*, 98, quoted in Neusner, *The Way of the Torah*, 23.
11. Estimate by Barrett, *IBMR*, 17.
12. Qur'an quotations are from the translation of A. J. Arberry, *The Koran Interpreted* (New York: Macmillan, 1974).
13. A. J. Arberry, *Sufism* (London: George Allen & Unwin Ltd., 1950), 42.
14. Al-Shádhilí, quoted in Constance Padwick, *Muslim Devotions* (London: S.P.C.K., 1961), 5.
15. Ibid.
16. *Atlantic*, Vol. 261 No. 4, April, 1988, 78, reviewing John Updike's novel entitled S.
17. Kenneth W. Morgan, *The Religion of the Hindus* (New York: The Ronald Press Co., 1953), 278. (Hereafter cited as *Hindus*.)
18. Ibid.
19. Ibid., 280.
20. Brihadaranyaka Upanishad I.3, *ibid.*, 318.
21. *Hinduism*, ed. Louis Renou (New York: George Braziller 1961), 119.
22. Ibid., 216.
23. Morgan, *Hindus*, 394, using Professor D. S. Sarma's translation. Cf. Juan Mascaro, tr., *Bagavad-Gita* (Baltimore: Penguin Books, 1962), 121: "Give thy mind to me, and give me thy heart, and thy sacrifice, and thy adoration. This is my Word of promise: for thou shalt in truth come to me, for thou art dear to me."

24. M. K. Gandhi, *Gandhi: An Autobiography* (Boston: Beacon Press, 1957), 504.
25. W. Theodore de Bary, ed., *Sources of Indian Tradition*, vol. 1 (New York: Columbia University Press, 1958), 354.
26. E. M. Layman, *Buddhism in America* (Chicago: Nelson Hall, 1976), 22.
27. Quotations from A. K. Commaraswamy, *Buddha and the Gospel of Buddhism*, revised edition (New York: Harper & Row, 1964), 18ff.
28. Ibid., 86.
29. Ibid., 95.
30. Richard Gard, ed., *Buddhism* (New York: George Braziller, Inc., 1961), 62ff.
31. Quoted by J. Kashyap, "Origin and Expansion of Buddhism," in K. W. Morgan, ed., *The Path of the Buddha* (New York: The Ronald Press Co., 1956), 5.
32. E. A. Burtt, *The Teachings of the Compassionate Buddha* (New York: Mentor, 1955), 211f.
33. Wing-Tsit Chan, tr., *Neo-Confucian Terms Explained: The Pei-hsi Tzu-i* (New York: Columbia University Press, 1986), 105.
34. H. J. Creel, *Confucius and the Chinese Way* (New York: Harper & Row, 1960), 123 (Hereafter cited as *Confucius*). I am grateful to P. Martinson for insights on the concept of intensification.
35. Holmes Welch, *Taoism: The Parting of the Way* (Boston: Beacon Press, 1965), 4. (Hereafter cited as *Taoism.*)
36. Welch, trans., *Tao Te Ching*, in *Taoism*, 64. Others translate "force" as "essence."
37. Creel, *Confucius*, 196, quoting *Chuang Tzu*.
38. Arthur Waley, tr., *Three Ways of Thought in Ancient China* (London: G. Allen & Unwin, 1919), 29f., quoting *Chuang Tzu*.
39. Lin Yutang, tr., *The Wisdom of Confucius* (New York: Random House, Inc., 1938), 104.
40. Creel, *Confucius*, 122.
41. Lin Yutang, *Confucius*, 105.
42. Ibid., 237f.
43. John B. Noss, *Man's Religions* (New York: Macmillan Co., 1967), 383, quoting the *Li Chi*.
44. Lin Yutang, *Confucius*, 237.
45. Robert E. Hume, *The World's Living Religions* (New York: Ch. Scribners Sons, 1955), 114 (Hereafter cited as *Religions*), quoting Mencius 2:1.1.23.
46. L. G. Thompson, *The Chinese Way in Religion* (Belmont, Calif.: Dickenson Pub. Co., 1973), 155.
47. Hume, *Religions*, 114.
48. Lin Yutang, *Confucius*, 162.
49. Some of these points are found in Joseph E. Brown, *The Spiritual Legacy of American Indians* (New York: Crossroad, 1982), 2-5 (hereafter cited as *Legacy*); Mircea Eliade, *Patterns in Comparative Religion* (New York: New American Library, Inc., 1954), 30-33; E. A. Nida, *Customs and Cultures* (New York: Harper & Row, 1963), 144.
50. Before proceeding farther let us note the problem of language. We have been using the words "North American" and "Indian" interchangeably to

avoid a problem that was created by Christopher Columbus. When Columbus reached the island shores of North America in 1492, he assumed he had arrived on the west coast of India, for which he had been searching. He therefore named the inhabitants *los Indios* or "Indians." Since that time, no one has quite succeeded in solving the confusion of language! The phrase "Indian religions" can refer to either the religions of India or to North American indigenous religions. Sam Gill, *Native American Traditions, Sources and Interpretations* (Belmont, Calif.: Wadsworth Pub. Co., 1983) (hereafter cited as *Traditions*), deals with the image-making of Indians from Columbus forward. It may be noted that in Canada Indians prefer not to use the term "natives" which is applied to part-Indians, or *Metis*.

51. E. H. Waugh and K. D. Prithipal, eds., *Native Indian Religious Traditions* (Waterloo: Wilfred Laurier University Press, 1977), 4. (Hereafter cited as *Religious Traditions*.)
52. Ibid., 18f.
53. Ruth Underhill, *Red Man's Religion* (Chicago: University of Chicago Press, 1965), 258, quoting James Mooney, "The Ghost Dance Religion and the Sioux Outbreak of 1890," in *14th Annual Report of the Bureau of American Ethnology, Part I* (Washington: Govt. Printing Office, 1896), 1085.
54. Quoted in *Christians in Service Newsletter* (Edmonton: Lutheran Association of Missionaries and Pilots), March,1988, n.p.
55. Diamond Jenness, "Canadian Indian Religion," in S. Crysdale and L. Wheatcroft, eds., *Religion in Canadian Society* (Toronto: Macmillan, 1976), 72. (Hereafter cited as "Indian Religion.")
56. Sam Gill, *Native American Religions* (Belmont, Calif.: Wadsworth Pub. Co., 1982), 32, quoting John (Fire) Lame Deer and R. Erdoes, *Lame Deer: Seeker of Visions* (New York: Simon & Shuster), 1972, n.p.
57. Cf. E. Washburn Hopkins, "Manitu," in *Encyclopaedia of Religion and Ethics*, 8: 402-405.
58. E. T. Seton and J. M. Seton, *The Gospel of the Redman* (Seaton Village, Santa Fe: John Seton, 1966), 21, quoting J. Fletcher, *Pawnee Hako, 22nd Annual Report of the Bureau of American Ethnology, Part II* (Washington: Govt. Printing Office, 1904), 347.
59. Brown, *Legacy*, 81.
60. Jennes, "Indian Religion," 73.
61. Gill, *Religions*, 68.
62. J. W. E. Newberry, "The Universe at Prayer," in Waugh, ed., *Religious Traditions*, 178.
63. *The Leader-Post*, Regina, Sat., July 16, 1988, 4.
64. Item C., page M-20, Saskatchewan Synod Convention, E.L.C.I.C., 1986, quoted by Charles Fox in unpublished "Polity Paper," 4.
65. *Christians in Service Newsletter.*

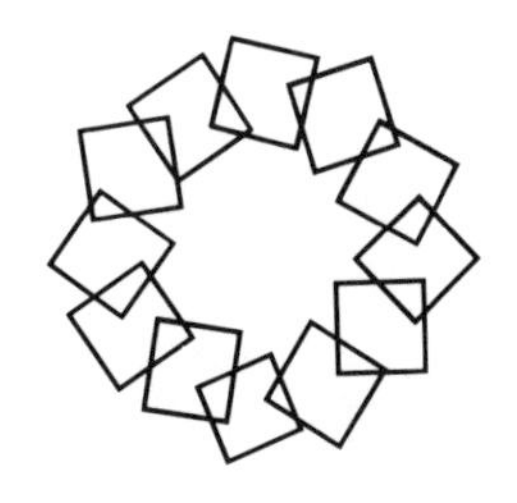

2

THE SENSE OF COMMUNITY IN ASIAN RELIGIONS

Wi Jo Kang

THE CHRISTIAN CHURCH AND NEIGHBORS OF ASIAN RELIGIONS

The biblical meaning of the Christian church is much more than a church building. The church is always an assembly of people, all kinds of people, transcending nationalities, ethnic boundaries, languages, and cultures. People of different backgrounds are brought together into the family of God by the power of the Holy Spirit through the means of grace, the Word, and sacraments. The church, therefore, is a faith community of diversified people who are justified by grace through faith in Jesus Christ. Apart from the presence of Jesus Christ and the justification of sinners who gather together in his name, there is no real Christian church. Dietrich Bonhoeffer was right on target when he wrote:

> The church is "Christ existing as the community;" Christ's presence consists in the world of justification. But since where Christ is the church is, the Word of justification gives reality to the

church, which means that it demands a coming together of the faithful.[1]

In this "coming together of the faithful," members of the Christian community are "no longer strangers and sojourners, but you are fellow citizens with the saints and members of the household of God" (Eph. 2:19-22). As fellow citizens in the same household of God, church members are to enjoy the grace of God without any distinctions or discriminations. St. Paul wrote to the Galatian Christians:

> For in Christ Jesus you are all children of God, through faith. For as many of you as were baptized into Christ have put on Christ. There is neither Jew nor Greek, there is neither slave nor free, there is neither male nor female; for you are all one in Christ Jesus (Galatians 3:26-28).

Missionary Mandate of the Church

However, this church, the united body of Christ, the community of the faithful, does not exist for itself. It has a distinct purpose to exist in and for the world. The church is to continue and to grow, not only strengthening those within the assembly of believers through the means of grace but also bringing others into that community of faith to share God's grace. Thus the church exists to further Christ's mission, and each member lives on earth to share his ministry of serving neighbors in love. Luther, in his commentary on 1 Peter, stressed this point:

> We live on earth for no other purpose than to be helpful to others. Otherwise it would be best for God to take away our breath and let us die as soon as we are baptized and have begun to believe. But He lets us live here in order that we may lead other people to believe, doing for them what He had done for us.[2]

Members of the Christian community are thus compelled to witness to God's truth in Christ in all human situations involving the needs of others. Christians cannot sit still while a neighbor is unjustly treated by an oppressive government, a neighbor suffers from poverty and deprivation, a neighbor is torn with despair and hopelessness. The followers of Christ are called to stand up and witness to the love, peace, and truth of God and then, led by the Spirit, to take appropriate actions in God's name. Above all, Christians are always to be eager to bring others to faith in Jesus Christ. This is the Christian vocation in the world. We cannot escape from it! Again Luther wrote:

> When a Christian begins to know Christ as his Lord and Saviour, who has redeemed him from death, and is brought into His dominion and heritage, his heart is thoroughly permeated by God; then he would like to help everybody attain this blessedness. For he has no greater joy than the treasured knowledge of Christ. So he begins to teach and exhort others, confesses and *commends his blessedness before everybody*, and sighs and prays that they, too *may come to this grace*. He has a restless spirit while enjoying rest supreme, that is, God's grace and peace. Therefore he cannot be quiet or idle but is forever struggling and striving with all his powers, as one living only to spread God's honor and praise farther among man . . .[3]

And Luther continued to insist that:

> [We] must not stop inviting guests to partake in this Paschal Lamb. But we must keep on preaching. We must also go to those to whom Christ has not been proclaimed. We must teach the people who have not known Christ, so that they, too, may be brought to the spiritual kingdom of Christ.[4]

In spite of Luther's strong emphasis on inviting "guests to partake in this Paschal Lamb," Lutherans in general have tended to be indifferent toward evangelistic outreach to people of differing races, cultures and religions. Their indifferent attitude toward Christian witness to others has been fostered by some theological positions of the past.

In the latter part of the sixteenth and throughout the seventeenth centuries, the world was rapidly changed by the exploration of recently discovered lands. Yet the followers of Luther were preoccupied with establishing doctrinal agreements at home to the point of almost forgetting the essential task of the church's life: to reach out to neighbors everywhere with Christ's gospel. John Gerhard, a representative theologian of seventeenth-century Lutheran orthodoxy, even went so far as to say that the task of mission had been essentially completed by the first apostles.[5] Such opinions certainly undergird the contemporary concept and attitude of many Lutherans who neglect reaching out to their neighbors in their communities.

Many Lutherans think that works of evangelistic outreach are to be carried on by specially trained persons such as missionaries or evangelists. Often Christians understand the missionary mandate of the church in the context of the word "mission," developed from the Latin word *missio,* which means "sending." However, sending specially trained people to witness the gospel of Christ to their neighbors, far and near, is only a small part of the missionary responsibility of the church. The Holy Scriptures include various forms of mission work. The New Testament describes the leavening aspect of Christian witness to everyone everywhere as an important responsibility of all members of the Christian community. Thus, every Christian, wherever and whenever he or she happens to be, is expected to share God's grace in Christ in words and deeds.

All human communities, whatever their religious traditions, are groaning for redemption. This is true as well, according to Paul, for all creation. Human beings everywhere, in addition to feeling alienated from God and from one another, are living under the threat of ecological pollution, chronic famine, and the threat of nuclear holocaust. The missionary mandate of the church compels us as Christians to help eliminate these threats to human existence and to enable everyone to live in reconciled community in peace and harmony, by proclaiming and actualizing God's good news of love, peace, and salvation in Christ to all our neighbors.

Now is a God-given *kairos*, a crucial moment in history for exciting ministries to happen. For the first time in history, the name of Christ has literally spread to all corners of the world. Indeed, there are rapidly growing Christian communities in Asia and Africa; many new immigrants to North America are already acquainted with the message of the Christian gospel and expect to live in a peaceful new community based on mutual understanding, caring, and cooperation. Christians can provide such a basis of human community.

Changing Communities

One notable change in the Christian church in America today is the decline of membership in Lutheran and other mainline congregations. Official church journals offer disturbing statistical evidence that church membership is decreasing. In 1986, for example, before the merger of the Association of Evangelical Lutheran Churches, the Lutheran Church in America, and the American Lutheran Church, each lost more than twelve thousand members. In its first issue *The Lutheran*, authoritative magazine of the new Evangelical Lutheran Church in America, explored the 1986 statistics. The analysis showed that the number of church members lost to death was 14 percent, and of those who departed to other denominations was 6 percent. However, the largest loss—50 percent—was through inactivity.[6] As long as inactive members remain inactive, the membership in the church will further decline.

Viewing this critical situation, some church leaders insist that the church that does not grow in membership is dead. We cannot agree with this point of view, for Christian ministry and life go on even in mainline church bodies that decline in membership. However, it is tragic when new opportunities to witness and to grow in membership are neglected by churches that do not take the missionary mandate seriously.

One challenging opportunity before us now involves the growing number of new immigrants, especially those who come from the non-Christian world. Many Lutheran churches seem to be waiting for new Norwegian, Swedish, and German immigrants to come and fill up empty pews. However, the color and languages of the new immigrants have changed the situation, perhaps forever.

The Asian population, with its diversified religious backgrounds (including Christianity) and languages, is increasing. Soon after 1965 when Congress passed the National Origins Act, Asian immigrants increased by 532 percent while European immigration declined by about 75 percent.[7] For the most part these Asian immigrants are finding their place in American life. In many urban areas, hospitals are now largely staffed by Asian doctors and nurses. Asians are among those who are renovating run-down urban areas to increase property values. However, Asians have not been readily accepted by their new U.S. neighbors. Less affluent immigrants may find themselves isolated in "Chinese towns" or "Korean towns." Asians who can afford to live in upper-middle-class suburbs still may have a difficult time mingling with their white neighbors. These associations tend to be superficial at best; at worst whites are openly hostile. While Asia traditionally has been the focus of intense missionary activity, generally Asian Christians are not welcomed into American church fellowships. Immigrant Asians who are seminary graduates have a hard time finding places to serve in the United States or in missionary positions of Lutheran churches. Perhaps this is one reason that Lutheran seminaries have difficulty in recruiting qualified Asians to study for ordained ministry.

It is hoped that the apparently insensitive and obviously confused attitudes of American Lutherans do not reflect the earlier, harsher attitudes toward Asians of some North American whites. For instance, in 1854, Horace Greeley of the *New York Tribune* wrote: "The Chinese are uncivilized, unclean and filthy beyond all conception without any of the higher domestic or social relations; lustful and sensual in their dispositions . . ."[8] In a similar vein, a California politician, writing in 1886, complained that:

> Whenever the Japanese have settled, their nests pollute the communities like the running sores of leprosy. They exist like the yellow, smoldering discarded butts in an over-full ashtray, filling the air with their loathsome smells, filling all those who have the misfortune to look upon them with a wholesome disgust and a desire to wash.[9]

Hopefully, such severe anti-Asian attitudes no longer exist. Christians should never reflect such hostile attitudes toward any ethnic group. That kind of hostility only alienates people further and hinders the Christian witness of love, justice, and salvation in Christ. However, the problem of acceptance is still present. It is not necessarily an anti-Asian attitude as much as it is simple aloofness on the part of many members of North American Christian communities toward their new Asian neighbors. Such an aloofness and indifferent attitude possessed by many white Lutherans is evident in the lack of Asian membership in most Lutheran congregations.

A Korean Lutheran pastor in New York City once told me that a person who phoned to inquire about the Lutheran church asked, "Is the Lutheran church a branch of the Mormon church?" The Korean pastor explained to him that the Lutheran church was the first and original Protestant church, that it has the largest Protestant membership in the world with a strong emphasis on biblical teachings. The inquirer then asked, "Why are the Lutheran people, then, not engaged in missionary outreach to Asian people?"

It developed that the inquirer came from an Asian country where the Lutheran church was not well-known, and thus he was unaware of the extent of Lutheran missionary outreach toward Asians there. Yet, we must acknowledge that many individual Lutherans do not make an effort to reach out in witness to the Asians of other faiths now living in their towns and cities with the Lutheran conviction of salvation through faith in Jesus Christ. The prevailing Lutheran attitude seems to be that "We have our religion, and they have their religion. Why bother?" Such lack of Christian concern is a disservice to our own great heritage and betrays our Lord's commission to teach and preach to all in order to make disciples of all nations.

Asian neighbors, like so many other new immigrants, are in the United States involuntarily. Wars and political and economic oppressions forced many of them to leave their homelands to search for new opportunities of life and peace in North America. They are seeking to find a new community, a place where they can belong. It is not easy, however, for them to find such a place of belonging because of their linguistic and cultural differences.

Those differences lead many North American Christians to see these new immigrants as strangers. Frequently the customs and cultures of the Asian immigrants are based on their religious backgrounds, and some Christians in North America tend to see these religions as "idolatrous" and "devilish." However, Asian religions really cannot be devilish if they provide the basic purpose and meaning of life for their people. A caring Christian approach to neighbors of another faith should not be to destroy their religious foundations of life. On the contrary, the Christian witness is to help them find a new community of faith in which cultural diversity is accepted as the enrichment of the whole human community. Therefore, members of Christian churches everywhere should take other people's religious beliefs seriously and treat them with respect. This means that in communicating the gospel to people of other faiths, the church should make every effort to contextualize its message. Contextualization of the gospel is not a compromise of Christian belief with the religious traditions of new immigrants. Rather, it is intended to make the communication of the gospel more effective through a better understanding of the religious background of the new neighbors. Contextualization does not change the central message of the gospel of Christ. However, it does acknowledge with appreciation the cultural richness of other people and tries to make the gospel meaningful in other settings and thought forms besides those shaped through the centuries by Western cultures and customs.

Through this process of contextualization, the Christian gospel contributes not only to the expansion of the Christian community of faith but also to the advancement of cultures. No cultural tradition is static in any given time and space. It is always changing, just as human communities are changing. The gospel of Christ, through which the Holy Spirit works, brings changes to individuals as well as to their collective cultural patterns in any given society. Many Asian immigrants to North America strongly seek such a change in their new lives, as they try to find a new accepting community to which they can belong. This is prompted not only by the situations they find in this new land, but also by the values they place on the collective life of human community. In Asian traditions, success and worth in human life come from belonging to a community rather than from accentuating individual greatness.

As Christians we value the community of faith and the collective importance of church life as an essential part of our witnessing the gospel. This should make us openly sympathetic to the emphasis on community in other religions. Let us look more closely at how these traditions view community. Perhaps a better understanding of what is vitally important to neighbors of other faiths will enable us to reach out to them more effectively.

MUSLIMS AND UMMAH

In Islam, the center of Muslim life is the community, called *ummah.* Muhammad, the founder of the Islamic faith, created the first *ummah* in Medina. He had gone there in 622 C.E. to escape persecution by his own tribe of Quraysh in Mecca. When Muhammad established the first Muslim community in Medina, religious and secular affairs were closely integrated. Muhammad was thus the secular head of this new community as well as its religious leader. The first mosque, the house of prayer, was not only the center of religious life but also the hub of educational, military, economic, and political affairs of the people who believed and submitted their total life to Allah. This community was further bonded together and sustained by the "Five Pillars" of religious duties:

- professing their faith in their creed: "There is no god but Allah and Muhammad is the Prophet of Allah,"
- praying five set times a day,
- giving alms for the support of the members of their community,
- fasting in the month of Ramadan,
- making a pilgrimage at least once in one's lifetime to Mecca.

By fulfilling these religious duties, Muslims express their solidarity and loyalty to each other. Thus the Muslim community is characterized "by a high degree of personal intimacy, emotional depth, moral commitment, social cohesion, and continuity in time."[10] Cohesion in the Muslim community is based on belief in Allah and respect for Muhammad, not on national origins, geographical areas, kinships, or occupations. The foundation of the Muslim community is *islam,* which means "surrendering" to the will of Allah.

As Surah X of the Qur'an indicates, "Mankind were but one community."[11] But Muslims who accepted Muhammad as the true and final prophet often separated from this "one community" of God to become the Muslim community of *ummah*, with hostility and arrogance toward other communities.

In their community, according to Muslims, dwells righteousness and decency of life. So the Qur'an states: "Let there be an UMMAH among you who invites goodness and enjoins right conduct and forbids indecency."[12] (Qur'an, Surah III.9.) Thus the *ummah* is the protector of human morality: "What is required of the community at large is likewise required of every individual member. This is because the whole community is an organic entity and every individual is accountable to Allah."[13] The Qur'an, in Surah IV:135, makes this clear:

> O ye who believe! Be ye staunch in justice, witness for Allah, even though it be against yourselves or (your) parents or (your) kindred, whether (the case be of) a rich man or a poor man, for Allah is nearer unto both (than ye are). So follow not passion lest ye lapse (from truth) and if ye lapse or fall away, then lo! Allah is ever informed of what ye do.[14]

The Muslim community is therefore characterized by a strong sense of justice, and justice is often expressed in supporting the general welfare of all its members. This is especially evident in the emphasis on the care of the widows and orphans. Sufferings and injustices inflicted on one member of the community are believed to be an injustice to all. Therefore, Muslims consider the welfare of their community a collective responsibility. It is their religious and secular duty to protect that welfare. If it becomes necessary to fulfill their responsibility, the members of Muslim community do so willingly. The *ummah* is sacred and any actions essential to protect it are among the highest and most honorable duties. To be sure, there are differences in the interpretation of that sense of duty among the various groups of Muslims. This is especially true between the Sunnis and Shiites. However, to participate in *jihad*, the holy war to protect Muslim communities, the sense of glorious martyrdom dying for the sake of Muslim community is prevalent in all divisions of Islam. For Muslims, there is no place of belonging more important than the UMMAH, where the life of Islam, the surrender to God, really happens.

Muslim *Ummah* and the Christian Church

Christians respect and admire the Muslims for their strong sense of loyalty and submission to the life of ummah and for their efforts to maintain a high standard of morality. However, any human community is an assembly of imperfect people, full of human shortcomings and weaknesses.

Christians also know that they are to submit their entire lives as individuals to the will of God, but they fail. Christians do, though, repent of their failures, guilt, and sinful way of life. Through repentance from sins and believing the atonement of Christ in the grace of God, Christians receive forgiveness. In that forgiveness they are called to be the people of God in Christian community and share the fellowship as equal members of that community.

Since the beginning of the church, Christian communities have brought together persons of diverse cultural backgrounds. We do not strive for the kind of uniformity such as that single universal Islamic culture which is generally common to all *ummah.* As in the first church in Jerusalem, we confess our faith and invite others to share the gospel in "their own tongue," satisfied to be united by that one faith in Christ. (Officially, the Qur'an is to be transmitted in Arabic and is not to be translated into the varieties of other languages.) Christians translate the revealed words of God for salvation for all people, so they might understand the Bible in their own languages. With the Holy Scriptures being available in a variety of languages throughout the world, Christian churches are able to sustain an exciting and creative diversity in worship, church polity, and architecture.

Muslims criticize the Christian church for being too hierarchical and for allowing the life of the church to be dominated by ordained clergy. The *ummah* has no "ordained clergy." It must be admitted that their criticisms are at times well founded. However, the ordained clergy in the Christian church are not called to exercise dominance over church life. Their tasks are simply to minister to people, to maintain efficient order, and to carry out God's mission in the world effectively. That mission is to bring the Good News of God's love, peace, and salvation in Christ to all people. In this mission of the church, lay members are also to participate actively in witnessing to the truth of God. Thus, clergy, the called and ordained servants of God, are not to be understood in any hierarchical sense but from the perspective of sharing the task.

The Church, Politics, and Power

Unlike the *ummah,* the Christian church does not identify its mission and existence so closely with the political, economic, and military aspects of daily life. Of course, Christians are concerned with the well-being of all the members of the societies in which they live and strive to work with others to achieve political and economic justice. However, having authentic political and economic concerns does not mean that the church has to have an army or an economic planning council, nor does it suggest that the community become a political entity, with its leaders exercising legislative, administrative, and judicial political powers. Even though some Christian groups have tried to do just that through the centuries, history reveals only failure, sometimes with devastating results. The Crusades provide a perfect example. Penitently, thoughtful Christians know that harnessing all of society together in no way brings about the kingdom of God for everyone.

Christ established God's kingdom not by political power but by fulfilling God's will through his sacrificial love and suffering. The kingdom of God is a gift of the Holy Spirit operative among all people through God's Word and sacraments. By the power of the Holy Spirit, people are brought into faith in Christ to believe in him as their Lord and King. In the community of faith, the kingdom of God exists and grows quietly. Since the existence of the kingdom of God is by the power of the Holy Spirit, the Christian community should not impose its will on other people. Ideally, even when the Christian community is threatened by external forces, Christians should be faithful to Christ first and suffer martyrdom if necessary rather than to justify *jihad*, a holy war.

Often throughout history, however, we Christians have misunderstood the nature of the church and its mission. Besides the crusading movements carried out against the Muslim world for control of the Holy Land, the church frequently engaged in the forceful extension of its community. Part of the problem was due to the close identification of the Christian community with the cultures and political power of the emerging European nations. Thus, amid their confusion of Christian community and their own culture, European Christians tried to convert nonbelievers to the European-Christian way of life by all kinds of coercion including military force. When nonbelievers did not accept Christ as Savior, the slaughtering of entire villages and the enslavement of people were justified. For this gross distortion of the gospel we, the members of the Christian community, still bear the shame. For we Christians do not live only for the perpetuation of the Christian community in human cultures. Rather, we live for the well-being of the wider human community by peaceful and loving witness to Christ's truth of salvation. In this spirit, we Christians are to meet and welcome our Muslim neighbors who are seeking a new community of understanding and caring.

COMMUNITY IN HINDUISM

In Hinduism the sense of the unity and oneness of human community is expressed in the doctrine of Vedanta, the system of philosophy derived from the Vedas. Vedanta teaches that all existing things derive their entity from a universal soul called Brahman. Each existing thing, including each human, has an individual soul called atman. Brahman and atman, however, are not separate entities but one. Only human ignorance sees them differently; the "enlightened one" knows the unity. The Upanishads, the Sacred Scripture of the sixth century B.C.E., explains the unity of all things in the form of a dialogue between a father and his son:

> Place this salt in water, and then wait on me in the morning. The son did as he was commanded. The father said to him: "Bring me the salt, which you placed in the water last night." The son having looked for it, found it not, for, of course, it was melted. The father said: "Taste it from the surface of the water. How is it?" The son replied, "It is salt." "Taste it from the bottom. How

> is it?" The son replied, "It is salt." The father said, "Throw it away and then wait on me." He did so; but salt exists forever. Then the father said, "Here also, in the body, forsooth, you do not perceive the truth, my son; but there indeed it is. That which is the subtle essence, in it all that exists has its self. It is the truth!"[15]

So the truth, like salt in water, is unseen; yet the truth is everywhere. One can taste the salt from the surface or bottom or center of the water. As salt melts in all water so truth permeates all things and therefore nothing exists apart from the origin of all existence. For the Hindu this origin of all existence is Brahman.

With this emphasis on oneness and unity, the Hindu community, like the Muslim community, does not distinguish between the spiritual and material or the religious and the secular realities of human community. However, in the Muslim community the commercial and political aspects of life play important roles; in the Hindu community spiritualism dominates. For Hindus political and economic concerns are subordinate to religious and spiritual requirements.

The Hindu community began to develop with the migration of the Aryans from the Caspian Sea area who settled along the Indus River about 1500 B.C.E. In the early days in this new land, the newcomers found a heavy emphasis on the offering of sacrifices, especially burnt offering of horses. However, some sacrifices did not bring about the expected results, such as healing of the sick, fortunes for an individual or a family, or a good harvest for farmers. This led the settlers to rely on seemingly better results that occurred when sacrificial offerings were made to gods by competent religious and spiritual leaders.

These religious leaders were called Brahmins, "the persons who pray." Brahmins were well versed in the Vedas, a collection of Aryan religious hymns and the basic text of the Hindu religion. Brahmins had knowledge about the attributes of the gods and were able to communicate with deities. Community life, centered around the priestly class of Brahmins, resulted in their becoming the dominant members of the Hindu society. A strict stratification of Indian society was beginning to take place.

Caste and Hindu Community

During the early years of the Hindu community's formation, political leaders and military generals dominated society. Later, by the end of the sixth century B.C.E., the generals and administrators formed the *Kshatriyas* caste, which is subordinate to the Brahmins. Then the conquered native people of the land, the Dravidians, became *Shudras*, those who would be on the bottom of the social stratification, or outcastes. Between the *Kshatriyas* and *Shudras*, farmers and merchants and common people formed the Vaishyas caste.

The caste system was finalized around the end of the sixth century or early part of the fifth century B.C.E., By then Brahmins had become so powerful that they were considered living deities who could even threaten, allure, or conjure spirits and other deities. Since the Brahmins possessed such power, their prestige and prominence in the Hindu community became unshakable. In earlier times in rural areas, when outcastes saw a Brahmin coming, they would turn their backs to the Brahmin and kneel until the Brahmin had walked a considerable distance away.

To outsiders, this rigid social stratification in the caste system appears to contradict or even violate the Hindu concept of the unity of human community and all things. However, to Hindus, the caste system is good because it provides a place and time of belonging for all human beings in their temporary worldly existence. Since individuals in the natural world derive their existence from the ultimate reality of the universal soul, Brahman, each individual human being—as an Atman is a part of Brahman—is therefore a part of the entire human family and the universal soul. As each existence is dependent on every other in the natural world, so in human community all human beings are interdependent and united as one.

Each caste social group is to fulfill its good karma (action) within the boundary of the caste, so that in a later stage of life or samsara (reincarnation) a soul can be born into a higher living being. Caste members, therefore, perform their karma as a kind of religious duty in the "givenness" of their caste. This ongoing activity witnesses to the fact that the human community consists of many individuals, groups, and castes, all of whom are united ultimately with one another as partakers of the one reality. In this way, the caste does provide a strong sense of belonging and continuity in a society. As Joseph Kitagawa writes:

> The caste provides an individual with a permanent body of association which controls every aspect of his actions from the cradle to the grave. The caste determines its own membership and maintains the continuity of skill, knowledge, and culture from one generation to the next. Despite the disadvantages and inequalities involved in the caste structure, no one can deny the historic role played by the caste system in welding into one community the various groups of diverse background in India.[16]

Christian Response to the Caste System

In spite of the Hindu tradition's strong emphasis on the unity of everything, including all of humanity, there is a rigid separation and discrimination among the castes in Indian society. This kind of separation leads to discriminations and mistreatments of humanity and even violence, despite professed acceptance of the Hindu doctrine of ahimsa (nonviolence). For instance, the taxi driver in New Delhi slows down when he sees a sacred cow roaming on the streets. Seldom, however, does the same driver slow down when a *dalit*, an outcaste, crosses the street. In Indian cities many Shudras and *dalits* live on the streets, without houses and often without food. Though these suffering persons struggle to survive under subhuman conditions, Hinduism seems to foster little concern for their welfare. In its sacred teachings, Hinduism does indeed emphasize the doctrine of ahimsa or non-violence, yet terrible violence is done to innocent children who happen to be born on the bottom or the margin of Indian society. These children must envy even the cows, because cows are often treated better than human beings.

With the development of cities, new industries, and modern education, there are hopeful signs that the traditional caste rigidities and separations are weakening. Now new social groupings according to new wealth, occupations, and education are emerging. Yet a strong sense of the need for separation and discriminations among the castes persists in many Hindu communities. In such a situation, Christian outreach to the people of India is understandably most successful among the outcastes. An overwhelming majority of Indian Christians belong to the outcastes. Herein lies the dilemma of the Christian mission to India. Since Christians are primarily those who live on the margin of Indian society, their witness to the gospel is not really breaking into the mainstream with much impact. However, as young Indians work to achieve their aspirations for freedom and equality, the rigid caste system will eventually break down. It may be then that the Christian population will rapidly increase in Indian society.

Meanwhile, many young Indian families are immigrating to North America, searching for freedom from the religious bondage of the caste system and looking for a new kind of community. These new Hindu neighbors, especially those of the low caste, are seeking a place of belonging where they can be accepted on an equal footing with other people. However, North American Christians often blunder by not reaching out warmly to welcome their Hindu neighbors. Provocative opportunities to share the gospel of Christ with newcomers open to new ideas are frequently lost.

Christians have much to share of their Christian faith and life with Hindus. By sharing a cup of tea and forming friendships, Christians would also learn from their new neighbors something of the reverence for life and deep spirituality that permeates Hindu life. Through the development of mutual neighborliness, Christians would witness to God's grace and mercy in Christ, thus enriching the spirituality and strong sense of human community that Hindus value. Above all, through such Christian outreach and dialogue, their Hindu neighbors may find a new meaning and purpose of life in Jesus Christ as they strive to discover a new community of human unity in a new land.

BUDDHISM AND HUMAN COMMUNITY

After Siddharta Gautama, the Prince of Lumbini who left his royal home in search of religious truth, had received his enlightenment or Buddhahood, he preached his first sermon at the Deer Park in Benares. He preached, "Now this, monks, is the noble truth of pain: birth is painful, old age is painful, sickness is painful, sorrow, lamentation, dejection, and despair are painful. Contact with unpleasant things is painful, not getting what one wishes is painful."[17] Buddha expressed his newfound religious truth in the word of *dukkha,* the suffering, which is inseparable from all existing things. This suffering is caused by the human desire to cling to the impermanent and illusory things of the world. The unenlightened soul continues to cling to the world of change and impermanence, and thus the pain and suffering in life continue. The nature of suffering in human community is eloquently explained in the Buddhist "Parable of the Mustard Seed":

> Gotami was her family name, but because she tired easily, she was called Kisa Gotami, or Frail Gotami. She was reborn at Savatthi in a poverty-stricken house. When she grew up, she married, going to the house of her husband's family to live. There, because she was the daughter of a poverty-stricken house, they treated her with contempt. After a time she gave birth to a son. Then they accorded her respect.
>
> But when that boy of hers was old enough to play and run hither and about, he died. Sorrow sprang up within her. Thought she: Since the birth of my son, I, who was once denied honor and respect in this very house, have received respect. These folk may even seek to cast my son away. Taking her son on her hip, she went about from one house door to another, saying: "Give me medicine for my son!"
>
> The Teacher, seeing that she was ripe for conversion, said: "You did well, Gotami, in coming hither for medicine. Go enter the city, make the rounds of the entire city, beginning at the beginning, and in whatever house no one has ever died, from that house fetch tiny grains of mustard seed."
>
> "Very well, reverend sir," said she. Delighted in heart, she entered within the city, and at the very first house said: "The Possessor of the Ten Forces bids me fetch tiny grains of mustard seed for medicine for my son. Give me tiny grains of mustard seed."
>
> "Alas! Gotami," said they, and brought and gave to her.
>
> "This particular seed I cannot take. In this house someone has died!"

"What say you, Gotami! Here it is impossible to count the dead!"

"Well then, enough! I'll not take it. The Possessor of the Ten Forces did not tell me to take mustard seed from a house where any one has ever died."

In this same way she went to the second house, and to the third. Thought she: In the entire city this must be the way! This the Buddha, full of compassion for the welfare of mankind, must have seen! Overcome with emotion, she went outside of the city, carried her son to the burning-ground, and holding him in her arms, said: "Dear little son, I thought that you alone had been overtaken by this thing which men call death. But you are not the only one death has overtaken. This is a law common to all mankind." So saying, she cast her son away in the burning-ground. Then she uttered the following stanza:

No village law, no law of market town,
No law of a single house is this—
Of all the world and all the worlds of
gods
This only is the Law, that all things
are impermanent.[18]

Understanding Community

As the parable indicates, ignorance about death causes greater suffering and tragedy than knowing that death is only a part of inevitable change in life. Therefore, for human community to be healthy, according to Buddhism, the members of the human community must free themselves from clinging to the world. Further they must achieve a state of nirvana. Like many other religious states of spiritual attainment, nirvana is difficult to explain. Nirvana literally means "extinguishing fire." Human life is surrounded by the fire of urges, selfish desires, and material clinging which causes suffering. To eliminate this suffering and achieve the state of nirvana, one must be released from the condition of worldly existence.

As Roland Miller pointed out, the way to achieve nirvana varies according to the different branches of Buddhism. However, all branches of Buddhism, even Mahayana Buddhism, which emphasizes the importance of family religious life, agree on the model of human community. This is the example of *samgha*, the monastic community. Those Buddhists who participate in the monastic life of *samgha* strive to eliminate the sufferings of human life and to help others attain the goal of the state of nirvana.

The Southern Buddhist tradition, often called Theravada or Hinayana Buddhism, developed in Sri Lanka, Burma, Thailand, Laos, and Kampuchea. Here great emphasis is put on the life in *samgha* with its observance of *vinaya*, the rules developed in *samgha* to preserve the truth of Buddha. With the emphasis on the observance of rules of *samgha*, the monastic communities become the center and ideal models of human community according to the Buddhists. There searchers of nirvana, who left the world of clinging, follow the way of Gautama Buddha to achieve high standards of morality in life. The life of *samgha*, as the ideal form of human community, prohibits the destruction of any form of life, stealing, unchastity, lying, the use of intoxicating drinks, eating between meals, attending secular entertainment, the use of jewelry, the use of luxurious beds, and selfish handling of money.[19]

The main part of life in *samgha* is the practice of contemplative meditation. The purpose of this practice of meditation is to cultivate the attitudes of the members of the community to feelings of loving-kindness, sympathy with all living beings, and compassion to all without partiality. The members of *samgha* are equal, although they recognize seniority and degrees of spiritual achievement. In any case, no one is superior to others or partial to another. Administrative decisions are made through a democratic process in which all members participate. Punishment for minor violations of community rules is often carried out collectively. For instance, when one member of the community does something wrong, everyone takes responsibility. There are exceptions, however. An individual guilty of unchastity, theft, or murder is expelled from the community.

Samgha is also a school where participants are taught reading and writing. In addition the school guides them in applying the whole ethical *vinaya*, or rules of life, to the wide variety of daily activities.

In other parts of Asia such as China, Korea, and Japan, Mahayana Buddhism puts an equal emphasis on the importance of *samgha.* Running through all of Mahayana Buddhist life is a vow to "take refuge in *samgha.*" The Mahayana Buddhists also believe that *samgha,* representing the assembly of Buddhists who have liberated themselves from the clinging to the world and sin, is the source of Buddhist truth. This is effectively the case whether Buddhists live in a monastic community or outside of it. In *samgha,* the nature of human community and moral life is both learned and taught. Thus in Mahayana countries *samgha* plays a vital role as the "enlightened community," center of the human community. This encourages everyone to strive for enlightenment in Buddhist truth. Thus in the life of all Buddhists, learning about the nature of human life as suffering and sharing compassion to lighten suffering are important elements. Thus *samgha* becomes the model of ideal human community where the peace and compassion is shared by all people. Regardless of the branch of Buddhism to which one belongs, Buddhist communities do not depart from their basic characteristic of helping to deliver humanity from suffering through exercising the life of compassion to others.

Several succinct sentences in Buddhist scripture describe the one who would follow *samgha* and promote the ideal form of human community:

> He abandons the killing of living things, lays aside the rise of a stick or a knife, and full of pity he dwells with compassion for the welfare of all living things.
>
> He abandons falsehood, and speaks the truth. He abandons slanderous speech, and does not tell what he has heard in one place to cause dissension elsewhere. He heals divisions and encourages friendships, delighting in concord and speaking which produces it.[20]

The Gospel and Human Suffering

Roland Miller finished his section on Buddhism with the question: "What is the good news in the gospel for Buddhists?" (See page 43). Perhaps one answer lies in the context of human suffering.

Christians, like Buddhists, take the fact of suffering in human life very seriously. However, Buddhists often say to Christians that while Christians may describe the world as "the valley of tears," they really do not accept the world in its entirety as the place of sorrow and suffering. As a result, according to Buddhists, Christians are often materialistic and this-worldly, still clinging to the world. Certainly we Christians recognize the existence of suffering and sorrow in the world. We also admit that suffering is certainly caused by "clinging" to the sinful world as the Buddhists claim, instead of clinging to God's truth. But Christians do see some positive values in the suffering facts of life.

Buddhists, like the followers of practically all other Asian religions and especially those Eastern religious cults active in North America, view human suffering totally in negative terms. Even the so-called Christian cult, the Unification Church, which originated in Korea, teaches that Jesus Christ did not come to the world to suffer and die on the cross, but to have a happy family and pleasant life.[21]

However, we Christians believe our Lord took the way of suffering and death to redeem the world, thus reconciling all people to God and to one another. The bitter suffering and death of Christ was an indelible expression of God's limitless love, offered freely so that whoever believes in Christ, as John 3:16 proclaims, "should not perish but have eternal life." Christ's suffering and death on the cross were truly unique events in the history of human spirituality. While Buddha meditated, received enlightenment, and taught about the suffering nature of human life and of human community, Christ actually gave the entirety of his life to the pain of suffering and death so that all humankind would have life eternal.

The followers of Christ are keenly aware of the fact that to follow Christ sometimes requires much suffering. Christ himself asked his disciples to take up their crosses (e.g., Matt. 10:38; 16:24; and parallels). Early Christians acknowledged such suffering as the price of discipleship. As St. Peter wrote in a stirring letter to early Christians in Asia Minor in the midst of severe persecution. "Beloved, do not be surprised at the fiery ordeal which comes upon you to prove you, as though something strange were happening to you. But rejoice in so far as you share Christ's sufferings, that you may also rejoice and be glad when his glory is revealed" (1 Peter 4:12-13).

Since Christ suffered for the redemption of the world, the sufferings of Christians in human community, in obedience to the life of Christ, are a form of sharing in Christ's suffering. In this sharing of the suffering of Christ, there are joy and happiness for Christians in this world. Christians are not counseled, therefore, to escape from the suffering of life, but courageously to accept whatever happens as a result of their proclaiming and living the gospel. In so doing they honor Christ's suffering way of reconciling the world unto God. Of course, Peter warned Christians not to suffer "as a murderer, or a thief, or a wrongdoer, or a mischief-maker; yet if one suffers as a Christian, let him not be ashamed, but under that name let him glorify God" (1 Peter 4:15-16). So Christian suffering, if necessary, has purpose. The purpose is to let the human community know that Christ's vicarious suffering for the forgiveness of the sins of the world is God reaching out to everyone.

Christians believe that all persons, regardless of their religious backgrounds or ethnic origins, are born in sin and estranged from God. For those who accept Christ as Lord, such sin and estrangement from God is, however, forgiven by God through the suffering and death of Christ. All Christians rejoice in the victory of the resurrection of Christ in the midst of suffering, affirming this great truth. Christ suffered, died, and rose again, fulfilling God's promise and love. Because of this love of God in Christ toward the world, Christians are prompted to love their neighbors as themselves. So the love of Christians toward their neighbors is also sacrificial, full of compassion and mercy. Christians and Buddhists both take the matter of compassion very seriously. However, Christians are to show their new Buddhist neighbors not only human compassion but also the compassionate outreach manifested in the divine love of Christ.

This divine love of Christ transcends all cultures, classes of people, ethnic distinctions, and sexual differences. However, in Buddhism certain discriminatory attitudes toward women exist in *samgha* and in Buddhist communities. Although Buddhism rejected the caste system of Hinduism and recognized the equality and importance of individual rights, often the female members of Buddhist communities are looked down upon and discriminated against. Ananda, a disciple of Gautama Buddha, once asked: "Master, why are women not allowed to attend public assemblies?" Then the Buddha answered: "With women truth is hard to find, to whom a lie is like the truth and the truth is like a lie." He also said, "Women anger easily, women are too passionate, women are envious, women are ignorant. That's why women have no place in public assemblies . . ."[22]

Buddhism also teaches that a woman who had really given up her sexual identity is no longer "woman" and able to be enlightened. Such a prejudicial attitude as Buddhism holds toward women does not have a place in Christian community. This is not to say that Christians never look down on women nor discriminate against the female members in Christian communities. However, in the inclusive nature of the church, Christians are to maintain their own identity, ethnic, sexual,and social; yet they are one in Christ who are all reconciled unto God. In this sense of the unity of humanity, Christians are to welcome Buddhist neighbors in their midst and share the dignity of human life in Christ's love, regardless of sexual differences. Sexuality is a gift of God in God's order of creation and should be celebrated. In fact the suffering aspect of human life is far greater among the women in any given society. Such burdens of sufferings imposed by exclusive and discriminatory attitudes must be lightened and eventually eliminated, by the sacrificial love of Christ extended by the Christians to their Buddhist neighbors.

CONFUCIANISM AND HUMAN FAMILY

Confucianism can be defined in two ways. One way is to understand it in a broad sense as a dominant Chinese religion and ideology together with all its practices. Another way is to define it in a narrower sense as the teachings of one particular historical person. Kung Fu Tzu, Master Kung, whose name was Latinized as Confucius (551-479 B.C.E.). These two definitions are closely related. Though the historical Master Kung was not an original thinker, he was successful in the systematizing of already existing Chinese ideas and popularizing related teachings.

Whoever studies the Confucian classics is impressed both by the strong emphasis on human-centeredness and this-worldliness, and by the pragmatic character of the Chinese mind. However, these impressions should not lead one to conclude that the Chinese denied the existence of gods, spirits, or other supernatural powers and thus lacked any religious dimensions in their lives. When we study the teachings of Confucius and his disciples we must always understand them in their historical and social context.

Confucius himself and other learned gentry were concerned primarily with human welfare in this world. They were not particularly interested in an afterlife nor with the welfare of the gods. Their concerns reflected important characteristics of the Chinese mentality in general. Hence, Confucius was not a theologian. He never intended to be and did not orient his teachings around the gods. He was a political and social reformer, with a strong sense of mission, seeking to bring order and concord in the seemingly chaotic period in which he lived.

Nevertheless, Confucius was a religious man, and his teachings are closely related to the religious life of his time. He recognized the existence of *t'ien* or heaven which was often used in an anthropomorphic sense as "heavenly being" or "the Lord above." This Lord Above, *Shang-ti,* is the one who watches and rules over human affairs and gives mandates. Confucius personally participated in religious ceremonies, using liturgical vestments and an accompaniment of religious music. (This tradition is faithfully kept in Korean Confucianism and less so in Chinese or Japanese practices.) The teachings of Confucius and his followers never minimized the religious rituals of Chinese life but in fact heightened it.

Family and Filial Piety

The disciples of Confucius gave ancestor worship the important place it has in Chinese religious life, making the family a religious unit and its head a "priest."[23] Thus in the Asian community influenced by Confucianism, the family is a sacred institution placed at the center of all things. The family values determine personal ethics and norms of living. In this family-centered community, filial piety of the children, expressed in reverence toward the elders and remembrance of the ancestors, is the basic foundation. Through the remembrance of ancestors, the children follow the wills of their parents, in whom they have the basis of their life.

Under Confucianism's strong emphasis on filial piety, the remembrance and worship of ancestors was institutionalized as a way of honoring the elders and the family. No one who wishes to be accepted as a legitimate and respectful member in any segment of Confucian society can escape practicing ancestral remembrance and honoring the elders. Thus the practices of filial piety and the proper rites of ancestral reverence are themes of the education of the young, and expressions of every individual belonging to a human community. Such practices of filial piety are so strong that no foreign religions or ideologies have been able to destroy the Confucian identity of the Chinese throughout their long history.

In the beginning of the seventeenth century, when Matteo Ricci, an Italian Jesuit missionary, came to Beijing, China, he observed that the highly developed culture of China was closely integrated with the rites of remembrance of ancestors. In fact, it was almost impossible to separate ancestors from the living members of a Chinese family. Ricci felt that Christianity could not influence Chinese society without some kind of Christian observance of ancestral rites. He became convinced that an observance of ancestral remembrance was a duty of all Chinese children and a responsibility of Christian citizens. Consequently he allowed his Chinese converts to practice the rites.[24]

However, the ancestral rites include a belief that "the ancestor is not entirely dead, that his soul continues to live and watch over the life of his descendants."[25] The rites also involve worship to these spirits other than God. Because of these elements in Confucian rites, Protestant missionaries in Asia were hostile toward ancestral remembrance. From the very beginning of their missions, Protestant missionaries in Asia deemed the practice of ancestral remembrance idolatry. Their leaders burned ancestral tablets and prohibited new converts' participation in any ancestral rites. Asian converts who received the sacraments were required to abandon the practice of ancestor rites altogether. An American missionary in Korea reported:

> When I was visiting a rural church to hold baptismal and communion worship, I examined a young man who wished to be baptized. He was the oldest son in the family and so I asked him what he was doing about the ancestral worship ceremonies which would automatically become his responsibility as the eldest son. He confessed that this was still an unsettled problem in his own Christian life, whereupon it was necessary to ask him to delay baptism until he had worked this out in his own mind.[26]

For anyone steeped in Chinese tradition, deciding to participate in the Christian sacraments and therefore to abandon the time-honored Confucian family rites is a hard choice. It means severance from his or her family. It is particularly difficult for the eldest son in a Chinese family. He bears a heavy responsibility for carrying out the duty of ancestral remembrance. If he avoids his responsibility, he is considered an undesirable member both of his family and of Confucian society as well. Such a person is also branded a destroyer of the order and harmony which all Confucian families strive to achieve. As a result he is treated as a bastard, an illegitimate child of his family, who ultimately does not belong to human community.

The Church and the Confucian Family

The biblical meaning of the Christian church, mentioned earlier, is not a church building but always an assembly of people. This assembly of people incorporates all kinds of people, even the "bastards" who are considered "destroyers" of order and harmony of a society. When Christ called his followers and through them formed the *ecclesia*, the people assembled included the misfits, the oppressed, the tax collectors, and other marginal persons of society. Social backgrounds and former ways of life became irrelevant factors among those being led by the Holy Spirit into the new family of God, the Christian church. In fact, marginal people who were mistreated in their former communities realized the greatness of God's mercy and love and became loyal members of the church.

The new faith in the Lord Jesus Christ generated by the power of the Holy Spirit gave people of different backgrounds a new sense of family solidarity in a new family of God. This was built solidly on the historical background of Jewish tradition which the Christian church inherited. Judaism always cherished the family solidarity that also reached out to embrace strangers. Edith Deen writes:

> In no other families in ancient world history was there such solidarity as was found in the early families of Israel. Each family was regarded as a community of persons and included father, mother, sons, daughters, brothers, sisters, grandparents and other kinsmen as well as servants. Included in the household also were "strangers within one's gates," sometimes concubines, as well as foster fathers and nursing mothers. All lived closely together, often in a tent settlement, probably like [the] small villages.[27]

It is the Christian intention to bring or accept all sinners and "bastards" in one family of God, where there is forgiveness of sins and eternal life through faith in Jesus Christ.

Christians should be able to appreciate the Confucian emphases on reverence of elders, remembrance of ancestors, and maintaining a strong order in both family and society. Similar to Confucian families, we Christians also consider important both ancestral lineage and the remembrance of our heritage. In fact it is an important part of Christian life. The Gospels of Matthew and Luke both provide a detailed tracing of our Lord's ancestral lineage. In the Lord's Supper, the remembrance of the one who gave his body and blood for the salvation of humankind is a significant element of the sacrament. Sometimes we Lutherans become so preoccupied with the notion of the "real presence" of the body and blood of our Lord in Holy Communion that we neglect this important aspect of remembrance. In fact the remembrance and the acknowledgment of the real presence of the body and blood of our Lord in his Supper should be inseparable. By the remembrance of our Lord who enacted the event at the

Last Supper with his disciples, we all share the same body and blood of our Lord with the saints who went before us.

As living members of the Christian community, we who now witness to the truth of Christ are carrying on the work of that great cloud of witnesses who passed through this world before us. Those saints are integral members of the Christian church triumphant, inheriting God's grace. Their faithful sharing of the gospel provides inspiring examples for their descendants. The creedal confession of "Communion of Saints" as synonymous with "the Holy Catholic Church" makes this vitality clear: The ancestors are alive and living members of the Church as the source of courage, evidence of their witness to the world and the hope of reunion in time eternal to glorify God. This great heritage of the faithful witness of the saints is kept as a treasure of memory for generations of Christians and as inspiring examples of witness in the Church.

How can Christians demonstrate that they too appreciate God's gift of family and more effectively share Christ's truth with their Confucian neighbors? To answer this question satisfactorily, it is essential that there be a greater participation of laity in Christian witness centered in family life. For a great many people, Christian life is confined within the church structure and dependent on the pastors of the church. However important the role of a congregation's pastor may be, Christian life is much more than church activities centered around a public location and a pastoral office. Indeed, Christian life suffers when the nurturing of the followers of our Lord is limited to the ministries of the clergy and occurs only within congregational buildings.

Surely the Lutheran doctrine of the priesthood of all believers must be evident in all phases of Christianity, including family and community life. This enables laity to participate actively in the sharing of God's love and mercy within the family through home Bible studies and worship. This is not to minimize the importance of the public office of ordained ministry, but to enhance and support the ministry of pastors.

A family is the basis of a society in any religious or cultural tradition. We believe it is God's design for all people to live in family structures where religious life would be nurtured. In the strong Israelite tradition, members of an entire family, wherever they went, built altars and worshiped God. All church activities, including public worship, should support and complement family life and assist each individual family in constructing and maintaining strong family bonds.

However, some Christians tend to separate religious life from the daily life of a family. They view their homes as secular or even profane institutions, acknowledging the church alone as sacred. Many Christian families today are unable to see the manifestation of the sacred within family activities and customs. Some in today's secularized Western world even look at the home as sacrilegious. The lack of dedicated ministry of the laity in family life is in fact a major factor contributing to such a distorted view of the Christian home.

It is important to remember that the Christian church originated in group meetings within the homes of the first Christians. Here converts, many of whom were strongly rooted in a Jewish background, gathered regularly for worship and nurture of their faith. For members of Jewish families, Israel's religious festivals were not only events for observance in their temples, but were broader celebrations within family groups. This was especially true of the Passover festival (Exod. 12:3-8). In home observance of religious festivals, every member of the Jewish family participated and celebrated. The Christian church needs to recover this emphasis from its Jewish roots. If Christian family members were encouraged to take part actively in worship, study, and observance of Christian celebrations at home, young and old alike would be prepared and inspired to participate in the broader ministry of the church's mission in the world. "Remember the days of old, consider the years of many generations . . ." (Deut. 32:7). Thus in Christian homes as in Confucian families, elders and parents would exercise their prominence and responsibility to lead family members to live daily in closer relationship with God. Such active participation of the laity in strengthening family life would be understood by the neighbors of Confucian heritage. Then the Christian witness to God's all-embracing grace in Christ to the Confucian community can be more effective.

In this youth-oriented, individualistic Western world, our respecting and remembering of family elders, our taking collective responsibility for the well-being of human community, and our actively participating in religious life within both family and the wider community are needed more than ever. Too much emphasis on the independence and privacy of individuals, combined with neglect of the collective needs of community life, is endangering the morality and sanity of society. Christian outreach to new neighbors is necessary not only to fulfill the mission mandate of our God to bring Christ to everyone, but also to build in God's name cohesive, healthy human communities, where all kinds of people live together in unity, harmony, and peace.

Any perceptive person, regardless of his or her religious persuasion, must surely realize that all human beings are imperfect, selfish, sinful, and at times destructive. Every one of us needs help from beyond ourselves to change. Ultimately, all members of the human community must learn to live together in mutual trust under the reign of God, with divine assurance of forgiveness of sin. The gospel is powerful in its simplicity: this reign of God is established through God's incarnate Son, Jesus Christ. Christ is for everyone the point of reconciliation, unity, and harmony in human community. This life of the communion of saints comes to us as a gift of the Holy Spirit, and as we are joined together in Christ, we can truly live as the "communion of saints."

The psalmist exults:

> Behold how good and pleasant it is when humans dwell in unity!
> It is like the precious oil upon the head,
> running down upon the beard . . .
> For there the Lord has commanded the blessing, life for evermore! (Psalm 133).

CHALLENGING QUESTIONS

A witnessing Christianity offers both the savior Jesus Christ and the community of his body, the church, to the world. How does this affect our identifying a core intuition of what Christianity is all about?

Absolutely central, of course, is the person and work of Jesus Christ. However, we must ask if anyone is really interested in Jesus, other than Christians themselves. Do other people want to see him? It is quite clear that the members of the major world religions are on the whole pleased with what they now have and are satisfied with what it gives them. They have an obvious pride in their respective religious heritages. Their sense of value is plain to all who maintain a living contact with adherents of other faiths, in Mainville or elsewhere in the world. Yet, this reality must be placed next to another equally impressive truth. The fact is that a sincere respect for Jesus Christ, and the desire "to see" him, is an almost universal phenomenon.

It is true that Christ's invitation to "follow me!" eventually produces a crisis of spirit for all those who perceive the meaning of his existence and the implications of his call. Yet, there is no doubt that his personality and message pass through traditional religious walls. It is as though he touches people at the very root of their religious instincts and speaks to their deepest aspirations. Jesus relates to each person in a particular and relevant way. He has a word for those who need to belong, to surrender, to be liberated, to extinguish suffering, to be harmonious, or to deal with powers. He is, indeed, the divine respondent to every true religious intuition. The "Greeks" who petitioned Philip, saying, "Sir, we would see Jesus," (John 12:20) were therefore really speaking for the entire religious world.

There are at least two major questions here. The first is how shall they see Jesus? What is the present-day Philip-Andrew linkage that leads people to the Savior? When he heard that the Greeks wanted to see him, one of the things that Jesus said was: "And I, when I am lifted up from the earth, will draw all . . . to myself (John 12:32). Thus the attractive qualities of Jesus and the prospect of being lifted up are joined together.

The second question is what will they see in Jesus? In the Gospels the words "And Jesus looked on them . . ." appear with great frequency. When Jesus' face is turned toward Jews, Muslims, Hindus, Buddhists, Confucians, Amerindians and all others, what do they see? Let us turn now to the consideration of that vital concern.

Notes

1. Dietrich Bonhoeffer, *The Communion of Saints* (New York: Harper and Row, 1963), 160.
2. Ewald M. Plass, ed., *What Luther Says* (St. Louis: Concordia Publishing House, 1959), 961.
3. Ibid., 959.
4. Ibid., 960.
5. Stephen Neill, *A History of Christian Missions* (New York: Penguin Books, 1964), 222.
6. *The Lutheran*, (Jan. 1988), 25.
7. David J. Frenchak, et al., eds., *Signs of the Kingdom in the Secular City* (Chicago: Covenant Press, 1984), 75.
8. Paul Jacobs, et al., *To Serve the Devil* (New York: Vantage Books, 1971), 93.
9. Ibid., 170.
10. Hammudah Abdalati, *Islam in Focus* (Brentwood, Maryland: American Trust Publications, 1975), 37 (Hereafter cited as *Islam*).
11. Muhammad M. Pickthall, trans., *The Glorious Quran* (New York: The Muslim World League, 1977), 200 (Hereafter cited as *Quran*).
12. Ibid., 60.
13. Abdalati, *Islam*, 38.
14. Pickthall, *Quran*, 94.
15. Nicol Macnicol, ed., *Hindu Scriptures* (London: Everyman's Library, 1963), 173.
16. Joseph M. Kitagawa, *Religions of the East* (Philadelphia: The Westminster Press, 1960), 134-35.
17. E. A. Burtt, ed., *The Teachings of the Compassionate Buddha* (New York: The New American Library, 1961), 30.
18. Ibid., 44-45.
19. P. V. Bapat, *Twenty-Five Hundred Years of Buddhism* (Delhi, India: The National Printing Works, 1959), 162-174.
20. Lucien Stryk, ed., *World of the Buddha: A Reader—From the Three Baskets to Modern Zen* (New York: Doubleday & Company, Inc.), 233-34.
21. *Divine Principle* (Washington, D.C.: The Holy Spirit Association for the Unification of World Christianity, 1973), 143.
22. Iwamoto Yutaka, *Bukkyo to Josei* (Buddhism and Women) (Tokyo: Daisan Bunmeisha, 1980), 181-189.
23. D. Howard Smith, "The Significance of Confucius for Religion," *History of Religions* 2, 2 (Winter, 1963): 242-55.
24. For an excellent treatment of this topic see George H. Dunne, S.J. *Generation of Giants* (South Bend: University of Notre Dame Press, 1962), 282-301.

25. Olga Lang, *Chinese Family and Society* (New Haven: Yale University Press, 1946), 18.
26. Allen D. Clark, *A History of the Church in Korea* (Seoul:The Christian Literature Society of Korea, 1971), 44.
27. Edith Deen, *Family Living in the Bible* (New York: Harper and Row, 1963), 20.

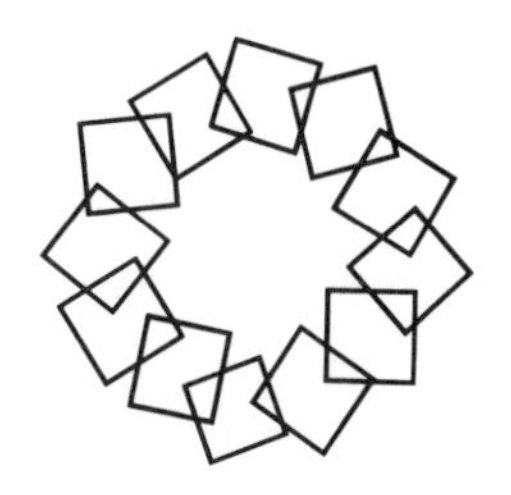

3

THE IDENTITY AND MEANING OF JESUS CHRIST

Carl E. Braaten

In his book, *Jesus Through the Centuries*,[1] Jaroslav Pelikan helps us see many faces of Jesus in the light of the general history of culture. In the setting of first-century Judaism, Jesus was seen as an eschatological prophet; in the revolutionary struggles of today's poor and powerless, Jesus is pictured as the liberator. During the intervening centuries we are confronted by a host of varied images. To the philosophical mind-set of Hellenism Jesus was the Logos, the rational principle of the universe. In Byzantine culture Jesus was the perfect icon of God and the inspiration of its art and architecture. In medieval times Jesus was depicted as the monk who rules the world through monastic discipline and self-denial. In mystical spirituality Jesus was the bridegroom of the soul; in the Reformation tradition, the Word of God who lives in the voice of the gospel; in liberal Protestantism, the perfect example of an enlightened system of morality.

Pelikan presents eighteen different pictures of Jesus down through the centuries, illustrating Albert Schweitzer's insight that each age pictures Jesus after its own image. In his epoch-making work, *The Quest of the Historical Jesus*, Schweitzer wrote:

> Each successive epoch of theology found its own thoughts in Jesus; that was, indeed, the only way in which it could make Him live. But it was not only each epoch that found its reflection in Jesus; each individual created Him in accordance with his own character. There is no historical task which so reveals a man's true self as the writing of a Life of Jesus.[2]

Schweitzer's rule is equally valid when we examine the images of Jesus beyond Christendom with their kaleidoscopic varieties of interpretation. Each world religion has its own view of Jesus in accordance with its peculiar vision of God and the world, of the self and salvation, of religion and morality. And not only the great religions but every sect or cult or movement places its own mantle of meaning on the figure of Jesus. To the Jews Jesus is a Jew, to the Muslims a Muslim. To the Jehovah's Witnesses and the Christian Scientists, Jesus is one of them. Or, Jesus is Black; Jesus is a yogi; Jesus is a freak; Jesus is gay; Jesus is *femina*; Jesus is the superstar of rock culture; Jesus is the guerrilla fighter. From the sublime to the ridiculous, Jesus is pictured as the perfect model of what each group intends to be.

JESUS OF NAZARETH AS A FIGURE OF WORLD HISTORY

When we look at the many pictures of Jesus in the history of culture and religion, we must conclude that he is a figure of world-historical significance. He cannot be kept the prisoner of Christianity, nor remain confined to official doctrines and liturgies of the Christian churches. His reputation exceeds by far the limits of those who profess to believe in his name and to follow his way. Jesus is, indeed, "the Man who belongs to the world."[3]

People of other faiths who have come into unfriendly contact with Christians still hold Jesus in high esteem. Evangelists and missionaries report from their experience that people are more interested in Jesus of Nazareth than in the religion he founded.

After 1900 years, there are still millions of people on this globe who want to hear about Jesus and to learn what can be truthfully known about his life and his meaning for our times.

The central topic for the agenda of the conversation of Christianity with other world religions has to do with the identity and meaning of Jesus Christ. This issue, of course, is also of most direct concern to Christians. Jesus himself first raised the question. On the way to a village in Caesarea Philippi, Jesus asked his disciples, "Who do people say that I am?" The disciples offered many current opinions and, just like today, there was certainly no consensus. Perhaps, they suggested, Jesus was John the Baptist, or Elijah, or one of the prophets, which is to say, someone who prepared the way for the coming of the Messiah. Then Jesus turned to his disciples and asked, "But who do you say that I am?" It was Peter who came back with the reply, "You are the Christ." And Jesus told them to keep it a secret (Mark 8:27-30).

Christian faith has built all of its beliefs, rituals, and institutions on the foundation of Peter's confession. All that is distinctive in Christian preaching and theology is centered in Jesus as the Christ. It is faith in Jesus as Christ that makes Christianity Christian.

Other religions share a belief in God. However, Jesus Christ is the Christian answer to the question, "*Which* God among all the gods of the universe do we believe?"

Other religions and ideologies have their paradigms of true humanity. Jesus of Nazareth is the Christian answer to the question concerning the true essence of human being and of being human. The identity and meaning of Jesus Christ is very much in dispute in the modern world. Christians confess that Jesus Christ is "truly divine and truly human." *Ecce deus, ecce homo!* The historical person and influence of Jesus of Nazareth continue to evoke from us the twofold confession: Jesus Christ is both God and a man, both the incarnate revelation of divine reality and the epiphany of a new and true humanity.

Today, Christians are being challenged to make sense of their confession in their contemporary encounters with other world religions, ideologies, and worldviews. The confession of the true divinity and humanity of Jesus Christ can no longer enjoy the security provided by the orthodox systems of traditional dogmatics. The confession will live in the world today, not as a function of remaining loyal to the creedal tradition of Christianity, but as a response to the challenge of the concrete person of Jesus of Nazareth. His reputation has spread far beyond the borders of Christendom. The modern search for the historical Jesus has exploded the traditional dogmatic and liturgical framework which tended to transform the concrete Gospel narratives about Jesus into abstract christological formulae. The *person* of world history became a *principle* of Christian theology. That has changed today. To quote Schweitzer again: "This dogma had first to be shattered before men could once more go out in quest of the historical Jesus, before they could even grasp the thought of his existence."[4]

The Bible is an open book that belongs to all of humanity. It is a book of history—the history of Israel, the history of Jesus, and the history of the early Christian mission to the nations—that can be investigated by historians around the world, whatever their religious or ideological commitment. Ordinary people as well as professional scholars are asking, "What can we know about Jesus of Nazareth?"

Dietrich Bonhoeffer posed the question, "Who is Christ, for us today?"[5] in one of the last letters he wrote before his martyrdom. It is an old question with a new vitality. People suspect that Jesus is more interesting than the religion people have made of him. A billion people alive today have been baptized into the name of Jesus, and many more than that are at least interested in talking about Jesus. How can Christians and persons of other faiths find common ground for meaningful discourse about the identity of Jesus? To begin with, all will be able to share the conceptions about Jesus they bring from their own traditions. But how can we all proceed beyond the kind of dialogue that merely results in a frank exchange of our various preconceived images of Jesus? We have already indicated that the multiplicity of images of Jesus has been created by a projection of particular self-understandings, each one picturing Jesus in accordance with its own character. How can we break out of this cycle of subjectivism and relativism, by which we can at best simply learn to tolerate, and perhaps even appreciate, the fantastic plurality of pictures hanging in the galleries of the world's cultures and religions?

The approach that seems most viable today is that of the historical method of interpretation. This approach provides a common ground, where we can all deal with the same sources and the same methods in working out our own contemporary answers to Jesus' original question, "And who do you say that I am?" Otherwise we are condemned to repeat the answers of the past without opening ourselves to the questions of today. If we or others are not open to a critical investigation of the identity of Jesus, utilizing the best tools of modern scholarship, there will be no serious dialogue beyond the preliminary round of interreligious and cross-cultural comparisons. It seems reasonable to hope that if Christians are willing to submit their confession of Jesus as Lord and Savior to a critical examination of the biblical sources, using the most sophisticated methods of historical research, then those who are not Christians should be expected to enter the dialogue on the same terms. The sources and the methods are public: They do not belong to Christians alone. They provide a mode of access to the historical Jesus that people of all persuasions can share equally.

We will have to concede that there are many Christians who will not wish to enter a dialogue with other religions concerning Jesus on such terms. Their view of the Bible as an infallible, inerrant, inspired book causes them to reject the historical-critical method. This is a problem internal to Christianity which we cannot enter into here. Our proposal for serious dialogue among the religions concerning Jesus is radically open to the historical method of interpretation. We see this as a direct implication of taking seriously the full humanity of Jesus.

The historical method does not, however, suffice of itself. It can, indeed, provide some objective control over rampant subjectivism that wants to recruit Jesus for some favorite cause. But on its own it cannot build a bridge to our contemporary situation. A hermeneutical factor must come into play, one that includes the dimension of personal experience, of belonging to a community of worship and witness, of following Jesus into the concrete world which entails service, suffering, and solidarity with sinners and victims. These are dimensions of Christian life that will never be fully contained within the framework of dialogue.

There is an element of truth in the subjectivist approach. Philip Melanchthon phrased it well: "To know Christ is to know his benefits." The fact that people picture Jesus in their own image is a symptom of the profound meaning he holds in their own existence. St. Athanasius and other theologians of the ancient church formulated this truth in the following way: "Jesus Christ became fully what we are in order that we might become fully what he is." Luther spoke of the relation between Christ and the Christian as "one cake." Paul Tillich, using the language of technical theology, made the same point: "Christology is a function of soteriology. The problem of soteriology creates the christological question and gives direction to the christological answer."[6] The approach, therefore, must be bipolar. Both historical and hermeneutical poles are equally essential in the construction of a christology at work in the dialogue with other religions.

Who was Jesus of Nazareth?

Not so long ago, theologians who were roughly identified as "the Bultmann school" combined historical skepticism with kerygmatic positivism to dismiss the quest of the historical Jesus as theologically irrelevant. Scraps of knowledge scholars might be able to glean from their historical Jesus-research were of no consequence to Christian faith. All that counted was the kerygmatic Christ, who lives as the risen Lord in the proclamation of the church. Today, the kerygmatic approach has given way to the persistent facts of history and the necessities of faith. Contemporary Jesus-research has demonstrated that we need not surrender to skepticism, nor may we retreat to dogmatism, postulating the self-sufficiency of faith over against the questions of fact. It is possible and important for historical scholarship to continue its search for the real Jesus of history and to construct an historically trustworthy picture of his public appearance, his message and ministry, and his way to the cross. Historians with or without any faith interest in the rabbi from Nazareth are able to pursue this research. And they must do so, given the commanding place that Jesus holds in world history. No explanation of the rise of Christianity is possible without reference to Jesus.

Furthermore, faith has an interest in the historicity of Jesus, and not merely in the interpretations which the early church passed on for its missionary purposes. It matters who this man was, what he intended, and what he accomplished; otherwise the church's interpretation would be empty. To embroider on a famous dictum of Immanuel Kant: Facts without interpretations are blind; interpretations without facts are empty. The confession of Jesus as the Christ is a combination of fact plus interpretation. The faith of the ordinary Christian assumes that the interpretation is grounded in fact and is not a free-floating construction of someone's creative imagination. God was incarnate in a person, a man of real flesh and blood, and not in an ecclesiastical dogma, metaphysical principle, or literary construction, although all of these vehicles may be used to interpret the significance of this event. It would be a devastating blow to the Christian movement in world history if suspicions would abound in the general public that Jesus of Nazareth never existed, or that with every advance of historical knowledge, traces of his existence would disappear into the sands of the past, leaving us with nothing more than a Christ-myth.

Contemporary Jesus-research has established beyond reasonable doubt that "it all began with Jesus." Jesus existed as an "eschatological prophet" within the framework of Judaism before the rise of Christianity. Knowledge about Jesus should be found in every world encyclopedia, and the article could be written with the same degree of historical accuracy as one would expect to find on Socrates or some other great personage of history. Courses on Jesus should be included in public school education, without fear of crossing the line of separation of church and state. Whatever we might include in such a course of instruction without using it as a tool of propaganda or evangelization might well serve as the initial core of our multicultural conversation about Jesus of Nazareth. That, I propose, is the place to start—with history and not with faith. It may happen, of course, that the impact of the historical Jesus may lead to faith in him as the Christ. That is a possibility beyond our control to make it happen. Faith is a gift of the Spirit, not a result of historical research.

The use of the historical method means that we cannot expect an exhaustive account of the life of Jesus, every detail of which is virtually certain. The nineteenth-century attempt to produce a historically trustworthy biography of Jesus has been abandoned in the twentieth century. The Gospels, our main sources of information about Jesus, do not lend themselves to biographical or psychological reconstructions.[7] Today, historical scholarship aims to give us a reliable picture of Jesus, the character of the man and his message. In this chapter we can at best offer a brief summary of a minimum of critically assured results and invite the reader to consult the works of present-day scholars such as Edward Schillebeeckx[8] and E. P. Sanders[9] for comprehensive summaries of modern Jesus-scholarship.

Jesus appeared in the popular mind as a prophet or rabbi, but neither of these titles is suited to his pronouncements and life-style. A prophet cries out, "Thus saith the Lord!" But Jesus said, "Truly *I* say unto you!" A rabbi interprets the Scriptures, appealing to their authority. But Jesus took authority unto himself and said, "You have heard it said of old, but I say unto you." He spoke with immediate and direct authority, not as one of the scribes or Pharisees. He seems to have been an unauthorized, lay, itinerant gadfly, holding no office, no title, no credentials. Yet, Jesus entered his public ministry with an astounding claim to authority, announcing the coming of God's rule in and through his words and actions.

The imminent approach of God's kingdom (rule or reign) was the nerve center of Jesus' proclamation. The kingdom of God is near at hand; for those who have eyes to see, its advance signs are already visible in his ministry. What is striking is that Jesus binds the coming of the kingdom to his own person. In a real sense Jesus belongs to the gospel he preached. In his own person he is the decisive event of its inauguration in world history, because the unconditional promise of eschatological salvation is actualized in his authority to forgive sins, to declare sinners acceptable in God's sight, to bless the poor and heal the sick. The relation of Jesus to the kingdom is so close that his death on the cross was seen as the enthronement of a king. Pinchas Lapide, a Jewish theologian, put it this way:

> Christianity is a who-religion; Judaism is a what-religion. Or, if you will, Judaism is a religion of redemption; Christianity one with a redeemer. For you Christians what is important is the redeemer, the king; for us it is the kingdom. We Jews know—under God—of a kingdom of heaven also, without a Savior-King; but we do not know a Savior-King without the kingdom already having come. Every morning television and the press confirm with terrible clarity that this world is not yet redeemed.[10]

Christians will have to agree that though the King has come, the kingdom has not yet arrived in its full power and glory. The world has not yet been transformed according to the apocalyptic revolution God had promised. Power struggles are still going on as always; the powers of sin, death, and the demonic continue to destroy human life and the whole creation. In fact, they crushed Jesus himself; he was put to death on the cross. So how is it possible to declare that the kingdom of God has come in the person and ministry of Jesus, when nothing apparently has changed in the world? Jews rightly have asked the question: "If the Messiah has come, why doesn't the world look different?" Christianity stands on this paradox: Faith declares that the decisive event of the world's salvation has already happened, the Savior has come; and yet, by all evidences, the world remains fundamentally the same. This paradox notwithstanding, Christians are asked to be prepared always to give an answer to those who ask for a reason of their hope in Christ (1 Peter 3:15).

The question is: Why do Christians confess Jesus to be King, Messiah, Lord, Savior, Son of God, indeed, "very God of very God?" What is the logic, the reason, of such titles bestowed on Jesus of Nazareth, whose life and ministry were terminated by death on the cross? The movement inspired by Jesus would not have made its way into world history apart from faith in Jesus as the resurrected Messiah. The resurrection event made it possible to believe in a hidden fulfillment of the kingdom of God in Jesus' ministry, his parables and miracles, and in his death on the cross. Simple people surrounding Jesus, twelve disciples, a few women and family members, some poor and oppressed people who had been touched by him, lived through the catastrophe of the crucifixion and before long went about proclaiming the "good news" that God had raised Jesus from the dead. This was the basis of the faith of the earliest Christians. Twentieth-century historians are not able to "prove" that God raised Jesus from the grave, but neither have they been able to offer a better explanation of the resurrection experiences of the first witnesses. Christianity stands and falls with faith in Jesus as the crucified and risen Christ of God. Here is the key to all the titles of honor and dignity that exalt the humiliated man of Nazareth.

On account of his resurrection, Jesus continued to be the leader of his followers after his death. Jesus was felt to be irreplaceable; he was their living Lord, the living Savior, the living Christ. He was present in the power of the Spirit, inspiring and leading them. There was no need to look for another like Jesus; there was no one who could possibly be his equal. He was greater than all the prophets, greater than Moses, Elijah, or even Abraham. Jesus was the fulfillment of what the faithful of Israel were hoping for; all the promises of Yahweh found their "Yes and Amen" in him (2 Cor. 1:20). In fact, he is the norm of good and evil; he is the criterion of truth and falsehood; he is the hope of the world; he is the power to change the world. In the end he will be the universal judge. The one who was rejected, betrayed, and murdered has been lifted up as the world's Lord and Savior.

The Christology that was in the making in the early church has had a long and oscillating history.[11] Starting "from below" with the lowly man Jesus, Christology moved to the highest possible identification of Jesus as God. However, the common assumption that the early church began with a "low Christology" and only later at Nicaea (325 C.E.) and Chalcedon (451 C.E.) developed a "high Christology" has proved untenable. Virtually from the beginning we have Thomas's confession to Jesus: "My Lord and my God!" (John 20:28). It could only have been with the utmost reluctance that a Jewish follower of Jesus would use such language, for monotheism was the hallmark of Judaism. Even more significant than the title was the place given to Jesus in the worship of the early Christians. Within a few years after his death and resurrection, worship and praise were offered to Jesus equal to the Father. If such language and behavior seem offensive to modern people, they must have been no less offensive to first-century Jews.

Today we cannot navigate the waters of interreligious dialogue without coming up against the "rock of offense" which is the place that Jesus holds in God's history with the world. Theologians who wish to de-emphasize or eliminate christological discourse in the religious dialogues about faith and theology in order to emphasize "what we all hold in common" are perhaps trying to salve the guilty conscience of Christians who want to repent of all the crimes committed against humanity in the name of Christ. They have coined the nasty term "Christofascism" to brand a theology which adamantly refuses to speak of God apart from the "God who was in Christ reconciling the world unto himself" (2 Cor. 5:19).

Such a Christ-less talk of God would seem empty of meaning and, in any case, not true to the specific Christian belief in God and hope for the world. In the dialogue between the religions, people have a desire and right to learn from one another the central affirmations of their respective faiths. Surely, Christ is at the center of Christian faith, from New Testament times to the present, because Jesus is not other than God. He is Immanuel, God with us—and not only for us, but for others, for all. How is it possible to believe this in a time when all religions have a right to be treated as equals?

We must be prepared to give a reason for the belief that Jesus means God for us. Perhaps most religions can quite readily revere Jesus as a prophet, as a religious founder and leader, as a martyr and hero, as a noble teacher and moral example. Jews and Muslims and Hindus and Buddhists can walk together with Jesus insofar as he is one of the prophets, revelations, avatars, or bodhisattvas. Every religion has reserved a special place for Jesus in its hierarchy of sacred names and symbols. The stone of stumbling is confronted while walking and talking with Jesus on the road to Emmaus, where Jesus revealed that he is the risen Messiah to which the Scriptures point. Emmaus triggered a chain reaction of consequences of incredible significance. This means that Jesus is the "eschatological watershed," the breakthrough in history of a new age of humanity, transcending everything that had ever been said or done before. He was a "new deal" and the "last word" concerning God's way with the world.

If this Jesus was truly God's own representative in history, his word was God's Word, his spirit God's Spirit. This was the assessment of the early believers in Jesus, and it is still the criterion of being a Christian today. Dialogue with the religions can proceed on many levels, beginning with our common interest in world peace, human rights, cultural enrichment, religious tolerance, ecological wisdom, and so forth. However, the dialogue will not become *theologically* creative without dealing with the deepest mysteries of our faiths. From a Christian perspective, the deepest mystery is not about some "God beyond God" who disappears into supra-essential nothingness (Pseudo-Dionysius, Meister Eckhart, Paul Tillich and others), but about the "God made flesh" who becomes fully and permanently embodied in the very humanity of Jesus.

Martin Luther contrasted two ways of thinking about God. One he called a "theology of glory," the other a "theology of the cross." Luther pitted his biblical theology of the cross against the philosophical speculations of scholastic theology. A theology of the cross must turn a theology of glory on its head, so that instead of climbing up the ladders of metaphysical, mystical, and moral self-salvation, searching for God at the level of the highest heaven, we see the human face of God in Jesus as we stand at the foot of his cross. There we find the crucified God in the depth of human suffering and alienation, in whom there is no "form or comeliness," not the glorious God that satisfies our intellectualistic and moralistic pride. The identity of God and the cross of Jesus have been welded together in history and in our faith, and they must not be separated in the witness Christians bring to their table conversations with people of other faiths.

On the Naming of Jesus

On the basis of such a close identification of God with Jesus of Nazareth, Jesus is no longer second in our scale of values. The decision for or against Jesus is a matter of life and death, a matter of ultimate concern. One decides either for the reality Jesus embodied, or against it. Jesus said, "No one can serve two masters." It is possible to give Jesus second place; then something else holds first place. What is it? It may be money or power or fame or career or self or the world or some such thing of relative importance. Luther said that your God is where you put your heart. This is what is involved in the naming of Jesus. Whatever a person has as another focal point of meaning and power for life, be it a cause, an ideal, an idol, or an ideology, will become a small letter "god."

It may be that Jesus redefines the reality of absolute meaning and unconditional validity. If this is so, then the particulars of Jesus' life and ministry invest radically new content into the word "God." It is not as though we already know all about God, then finding such a likeness of this idea of God in Jesus, we are finally prepared to say God-like things about Jesus. It is the other way around. Jesus specifies who and what we mean by "God." To say to Jesus, "My Lord and my God," means to let his historical appearance reveal God to us and thus change our understanding of God.

This is not to claim that the God revealed in Jesus is different from the God at work throughout the world and all the religions of humankind. It does mean that Christian theologians interpret the God of Abraham, Isaac, and Jacob, as well as the "unknown God" of Hellenistic religion, in light of the story of Jesus and his love. When we hear and believe the gospel, we know what God is like, and that God is therefore totally compassionate toward all people. None are excluded. Such a love is the strongest power in the world and will conquer all things in the end. This is the love of the suffering servant who, disinterested in rank, honor, and status at the top of the social pyramid, lays down his life for others. God's love totally expressed itself in Jesus' solidarity with the poor and weak. Here is not an ascending love that detaches itself from the real world of human suffering; it is a descending love that seeks the liberation of all people and the transformation of the world. How can we know now that this is the true and final self-revelation of God? What makes it normative in our Christian interpretation of human existence and communal experience? We can only test this idea like the proverbial tree, by its fruits. Apart from firsthand experience of God's conquering love, apart from the impact of Jesus in the lives of those who need him, there is no proof at all.

Jesus of Nazareth is the historical link between Jews and Christians. The God whom Jesus called his Father was the God of Israel. Jews are blood brothers and sisters of Jesus, coming from the same household of faith. Gentiles have been adopted into this same family through their faith in Jesus as the Messiah of Israel. Thus, Jews and Gentiles alike are sons and daughters of their father Abraham. The history of God with Israel took on a new beginning when Jesus commissioned his apostles to spread the good news of the kingdom to all the nations. Hence, all the nations that have heard the gospel through the history of the apostolic mission have been drawn into the one history of God with Israel and Jesus of Nazareth. And the Bible has become their sacred Scriptures by way of adoption.

The gospel is the announcement that God in Christ is drawing all people unto God. The God of Israel and the Father of Jesus Christ is none other than the God at work in all religions as the power of their origin and destiny. This is a direct implication of biblical monotheism. Religions live and move and have their being in the stream of history. There they all inevitably come into contact with the Christian movement that announces to them a new and unexpected future beyond their own way of ordering the world. As a religion, Christianity does not proclaim itself as the universal unity of humankind. However, the task of the Christian mission is to mediate the knowledge of a unity that God is in the process of creating through the proclamation of the gospel. If Christians did not believe this, the mission of the gospel in world history would come to an end, and the revelation of God's universal plan according to the Scriptures would be aborted. But that is an impossible thought for the faithful.

The history of the Christian mission has demonstrated an openness to new ways of proclaiming the gospel. There are always new ways of naming Jesus in light of particular religious and cultural contexts to which the message is addressed. From one perspective, Christianity looks like a chameleon, reflecting the local color of each cultural context which its message penetrates. There is a true sense in which every concrete manifestation of the Christian faith is syncretist, and inevitably so. Just as many religions have gone into the making of historic Christianity, so also is Christianity drawing them into its own orbit of spiritual history. Such historical interaction continues today through evangelization, mission, dialogue, and service. Through all the variables the constant factor, as we have emphasized, is the message concerning God's final saving revelation in Jesus Christ. So, far from closing Christianity to other religions, it is this message of Christ that opens Christianity to all the highways and byways of the religious history of humanity. God has not been without witnesses anywhere in the world; God is at work in all the religions of humankind, preparing them for a future when they will confess the "way, the truth and the life" revealed in Jesus. Wise Men from the East—and from all corners of the world—have brought their gifts to celebrate the advent of God's kingdom in the person of Jesus.

The history of Christology remains open. New ways of naming Jesus as the saving act of God in world history will be found as the gospel continues to incarnate itself in each and every indigenous culture. Pluralism is nothing new; neither is the awareness of this phenomenon. Israel first, and then Christianity, have always been surrounded by a host of other religious symbols, rituals, and divinities. One approach is simply to negate all of these as the "wiles and ways of the devil." The opposite approach is to equate all of them with the revelation of God in Jesus Christ. A mediating approach seems more viable in light of the Scriptures and the history of the Christian mission. We might call this a dialectical method of interpretation, which looks for new ways of interpreting the meaning of Christ in the language and symbols of other nations, cultures, and religions in the whole of God's creation. Beyond the pages of the Bible and outside the walls of the church there are, as Karl Barth said, "parables of the kingdom."[12] These constitute a third circle of witnesses, including words and signs and lights and revelations which say materially the same thing as the Scriptures attest concerning the one and only Word of God in Jesus Christ, "although from a different source and from another tongue."[13] The Christian community must listen to these other witnesses for whatever they say about truth and reality, believing that in the end they must illumine, accentuate, and help to explicate the truth and reality of God incarnate in Jesus Christ.

Our dialectical interpretation is based on the belief that the God who is redeeming the world in Jesus Christ is none other than the God who is creating the world out of nothing. The first, second, and third articles of the Apostles' Creed speak of the same God—Creator, Redeemer, and Sanctifier. A dialectical view rules out the two models of interpretation to which we have just referred. The first thinks of *delivering* Christ to the nations as into a void, with a firm sense of Christ being totally absent. The second thinks of *discovering* Christ in the symbols and rituals of a given religion, with theexpectation of finding Christ already there. Both of these are nondialectical. A dialectically conceived Christian theology of the world religions may search for the religious symbols that seem to anticipate in some way the light of the gospel that draws all people to see the revelation of God in Jesus Christ. The translation of the Bible and the proclamation of the gospel in all world languages presuppose a certain continuity between the revelation of God in various religions and God's revelation in Jesus Christ. A deep translation of the Christian message must enter into the constitutive symbolism of other religious traditions and discover their liveliest symbols of salvation. If Jesus is to find a home in all cultures and religions, he must be experienced as Savior at the core of every religious quest for salvation. This means taking the risk of finding new ways of naming Jesus, or rather, taking the old symbols in each religion and saying something new through them.

The New Testament is our best example of how old language, the language of Israel's religious traditions, was adopted, converted, and baptized in the process of declaring the Word of God in Jesus Christ. The cross of Jesus transforms the meaning of preexistent symbols. If Jesus is called the "Lamb of God," Jesus' own suffering and death on the cross invest that symbol with new meaning. There is continuity, but also discontinuity. In light of Jesus' own praxis, he changes the meaning of "King," "Lord," "Messiah," "Logos," "Son of God," "Savior," "High Priest," and all the other names and symbols taken from Judaism and Hellenism to identify him. He transvaluates them all, turns them upside down. The King stoops down to become a common citizen; the Lord becomes the lowliest servant; the Messiah saves from the cross; the Logos is a person; the High Priest becomes the sacrificial lamb. Status and rank are axiomatically reversed. "Many that are first will be last, and the last first" (Mark 10:31). "For what is exalted among men is an abomination in the sight of God" (Luke 16:15). Let the leaders become humble servants. The backs of hierarchical models of religion, culture, and politics are broken with such a reversal of roles.

In light of the feminist protest against the patriarchal Father-God, it is particularly important to emphasize today that Jesus changes the shape and content of the idea of God. The attack on "God the Father" is really directed against the pyramidal hierarchical system over which this Lord-God presides. "He" presides at the top of the pyramid. Thus, there is a celestial hierarchy eternally pre-establishing the order of the earthly hierarchy. At the bottom is the family unit, with the *paterfamilias* owning his wives and children and servants and cattle. At the next level is the Fatherland, with the *paterpatriae* ruling over the nation like a father his family. On the next plane there are religious authorities; they are called "church fathers," and the mothers are out of sight. At the top of the ecclesiastical hierarchy sits the Holy Father. This patriarchal Father-God has become the reigning figure of Jewish, Muslim, and Christian monotheism. Jewish-Christian monotheism allied itself with Hellenistic philosophical monism, as well as with the political monarchism of imperial Rome. Religion, philosophy, and politics were constituent parts of an oppressive patriarchal synthesis topped off by the image of God as Almighty Father.

The Father of Jesus Christ is not synonymous with the God of the patriarchal system, religious monotheism, or political monarchism. As Elisabeth Schussler Fiorenza has shown,[14] the revelation of God focused in Jesus breaks away from patriarchal religion and culture, in that Jesus founded a discipleship community of equals. Jesus' vision of the kingdom of God calls for a praxis of inclusive wholeness as an alternative option to the dominant patriarchal structures. The early church was a countercultural egalitarian movement. In principle the church challenged the conventional power arrangements and provided liberating experience to those who were victims of the system on account of their gender, race, social status, or whatever. As Robert Hammerton-Kelly has argued in *God the Father*,[15] Jesus' address to God as "Abba" destabilized the traditional patriarchal model, because its model of mutuality, intimacy, and love had the effect of establishing a community in which all persons, regardless of their worldly rank, could assemble as equals.

How Other Religions See Jesus

We have observed how the early church confessed the risen Jesus, ascribing titles of honor and dignity that underscored the uniqueness and universality of his saving work. We have shown how the christological titles taken from the world of Jewish or Hellenistic religion were transformed in their application to Jesus. A familiar symbol with a meaning already known such as Logos or Kyrios became filled with a new content in its Christian appropriation, to become a further naming of the One whose name "is above every name" (Phil. 2:9), the supername of Jesus.

In the post-apostolic church, the classic paradigm for this process of naming Jesus was the use of the Logos concept. In its simplest meaning, Logos means "word." But in Hellenistic philosophy the Logos referred both to the rational structure of reality and the rational structure of the mind, to what makes knowledge possible. This concept expressed the universal manifestation of divine reality in the whole cosmos, ordering it and giving it meaning. The church fathers took this metaphysical principle and applied it to the concrete personal life of Jesus, the incarnation of God in human flesh. Thus they drew the Logos into a new field of meaning. They explained that seeds of the Logos, already planted throughout the cosmos, were preparations for the definitive appearance of the Logos in the historical person of Jesus Christ.

The extension of Christology in this new direction was a step the ancient church had to take, to speak of Christ in the context of Hellenistic religion. It would have been meaningless to explain the gospel in the old "language of Canaan." But it was a step that involved a risk. The danger was that Jesus Christ would be seen as a middle thing between God and humanity. In Hellenistic philosophy the Logos was exactly such a middle thing, mediating between the One (God) and the many (the world). That would be inadequate to express the Christian belief in Jesus as Savior, for the true mediator of salvation cannot be half-divine and half-human, some third thing between God and humanity. Struggling to avoid the danger of making Jesus into a near-divinity, the ancient councils of the church finally stated the paradox that Jesus Christ is truly God, homogeneous with the Father, and truly human, equally homogeneous with essential humanity.

Today, Christian theology must take similar risks in contextualizing its language about God and Jesus. The examples of the New Testament community and of the ancient church will always remain the classic paradigms instructing new communities of faith on how to interpret the old faith in new symbols. The dialectical process of interpretation continues today on every continent and island, in every culture and language.

Christianity began in an age of religious pluralism and it finds itself today in a similar situation, only intensified by the fact that there are so many challenges on so many different fronts at once. Some theologians, such as John Hick and Paul Knitter, feel the present situation is so utterly novel that it spells the end of the classic paradigms of interpretation. They speak of a "Copernican revolution" in which Christ is removed from the center of Christian faith as well as from the center of the Christian theology of the religions. I believe that their suggested break in continuity with the classic traditions of Christian faith is suicidal. In fact, it means a conversion from the christological center of faith to some other center to define what is constitutive and normative for theology and religion.

As a step in the direction of a positive christological interpretation of other religions, it is important and useful to ask about how other religions see Jesus. This may help us to get at the soteriological center, the core intuition, of each religion with the hope that we will find symbols waiting to express and celebrate the salvation which God wills to mediate to all peoples and cultures "in the name of Jesus."

Judaism. Something exciting is happening today that has never happened since the original schism between Judaism and Christianity. We are witnessing the process of a recovery of Christianity's Hebrew roots as well as a Jewish recovery of Jesus. Pinchas Lapide refers to this process as "*Heimholung*"[16] ("bringing home"). He speaks of a "Jesus wave," citing "the 198 Hebrew books, research articles, poems, plays, monographs, dissertations, and essays that have been written about Jesus in the last twenty-seven years since the foundation of the state of Israel."[17] Jewish scholars participate with Christian scholars in the new quest of the historical Jesus, reaching the unavoidable conclusion that whatever else he was, Jesus was a Jew.

As Christians are working on a more adequate Christian theology of Judaism, so Jews are reciprocating with a Jewish theology of Christianity. The common ground of Judaism and Christianity is considerable; both are messianic religions. Jesus is a bond on union between all Jews and Gentiles who confess faith in Yahweh whom Jesus addressed as "Abba." In addition to Yahweh and Jesus, Jews and Christians are paradoxically most deeply united by the beliefs that divide them, such as, belief in the Messiah, the coming of the kingdom, and resurrection beyond death. Jews are still waiting for the coming of the Messiah and the establishment of the reign of God. Christians believe that the Messiah has already come and has established "a kingdom not of this world" through his cross and resurrection. Jews expected the resurrection as an eschatological event of the last days which Christians believe had already begun to happen in Jesus' resurrection from the dead—the "first fruits."

Who was Jesus of Nazareth, then, if he was not the long-awaited Messiah of Israel? And why do Jews honestly refuse to accept Jesus as the Messiah? There is, of course, no consensus among Jewish scholars in answering these questions. But, all would agree at least to this: If Jesus had been the Messiah, the prophecies of old would have been fulfilled and the coming of the kingdom would be apparent. But this is obviously not the case, for the world has not been changed in any dramatic way, not as long as there is genocide, racism, violence, war, poverty, hunger, and the like. When the Messiah brings in the kingdom, there will be an era of peace, righteousness, and fulfillment for all humanity and the world. Jews are still waiting for the coming of the Messiah and the dawn of a new age. Nevertheless, Jews can accept Jesus as a prophet in the history of salvation, as a pre-eschatological event preparing the way, like other prophets, for the coming of the Messiah. From a Jewish eschatological perspective there is nothing decisive, definitive, final, normative, and exclusive about the appearance of Jesus of Nazareth. Yet, Jesus may be accepted as one in the line of the patriarchs and prophets of Israel pioneering the full salvation of the future kingdom which God will establish through the Messiah in the last days.

From a Jewish perspective, then, the world-historical significance of Jesus is that he became the occasion to release the particularism of Judaism into the stream of universal history by way of the Gentile mission. As Franz Rosenzweig stated in *The Star of Redemption*,[18] the nations of the world could become heirs of Jewish monotheism only on the condition of the Jewish refusal of the gospel. Jews may see Christianity, in its deepest aim and intention to convert the world to the One God, as the Judaizing of the Gentiles. Christianity and Judaism are two different forms of monotheism. However, on the basis of the Christ-event, Christians are trinitarian monotheists, perhaps "odd monotheists" but certainly not tritheists. The Christian gospel brings the knowledge of the Father into the world of the Gentiles, and thus the Christian church functions as an institution of salvation alongside of Israel for the sake of all the nations. Thus, Christianity has salvation-historical meaning, if not for the Jews, then for the wider Gentile world.

Jews will go on praying for the coming of the Messiah; Christians will continue to pray to the Messiah who has already come. There is that decisive difference. Yet, it is a difference that presupposes an underlying unity. On the basis of his first advent, Jesus is proclaimed as the Savior of all the Gentiles; in his final parousia Jesus will manifest himself also as the Messiah of Israel. On account of the standing of Jesus in the plan of God for the world's salvation, there is no ultimate separation between Israel and the church. This seems to be the clear message of Paul in Romans 9–11.

Islam. Unlike the Hebrew Bible, Islam's sacred book, the Qur'an, contains an explicit Christology. The Qur'an speaks of Jesus in many passages, always in a positive light. However strained the relations between Christians and Muslims have been, the figure of Jesus as a prophet and messenger of God, even as a suffering servant of God, provides a point of contact that goes deeper than their mutual recriminations. Before Christian theologians engage in apologetics or polemics in attempting to prove the truth of the biblical view of Christ, it is necessary for them to give sympathetic attention to the Muslim view of Jesus in the Qur'an.

The first thing that looms up is the great divide between God and Jesus. Karl Barth's famous utterance, "God is in heaven and man is on earth," would be fully acceptable to Muslims. The cardinal sin for Islam is "*Shirk*," a word that means "associating" something with God, giving God a partner on the same level. What Muslims hear Christians saying about the divinity of Christ and the Trinity sounds like blatant idolatry. Against all such is the Qur'anic version of the First Commandment: *La ilaha illa Allah* ("Exalted be Allah above all that they associate.") In Islam Jesus must not be elevated to the level of the divinity. Jesus is a man and not more than human, albeit one of the great prophets of God along with Abraham, Noah, and Moses. All of these are precursors of Muhammad, the last and greatest prophet of Allah.

Once Jesus' creaturely status is guaranteed, the Qur'an has some interesting things to say about his prophetic role and destiny. Jesus is declared to be the Word or Truth or Spirit of God, all titles which we find in the New Testament. Jesus is one sent by God, a "*rasul*," a messenger. There are only four *rasul* acknowledged by Islam: Moses, David, Jesus, and Muhammad.

To the extent that the one who is sent is an authentic representative of the One who sends, some kind of unity must be acknowledged that mediates the duality. There must be a revelational unity, then, inherent in the message of God coming through the messenger. So, ultimately, God is not only "in heaven" but must be present "on earth" in some modality, wherever a community receives and grasps the revealing word and will of God.

Christians, no doubt, want to say more about the unity of God and Jesus, the paradox at the heart of the gospel. For Christians the personal union of Jesus with his Father becomes the root of the doctrine of the Trinity. For Muslims such a personal union drives Christians into what looks like tritheism. The Qur'an says: "They are unbelievers who say God is threefold. No god there is but One God" (Sura 5, 78). For Christians, too, Jesus is a prophet, but more than a prophet, since he assumed God's authority, forgave sins, and fulfilled the law and the prophets.

Liberal Protestantism reflects early Jewish Christianity with its "low Christology" and comes very close to expressing what Muslims say about Jesus. Some scholars think that, in fact, the "low Christology" of early Jewish Christianity, which saw Jesus as a "mere man" and at best a great prophet and servant of God, survived in its basic structure in Islamic Christology. This old Syriac-Semitic Christology was condemned as heretical in the early church councils, with their anathemas against ebionitism, adoptionism, modalistic monarchianism, and Nestorianism. With the spread of Christianity into the Hellenistic world of thought, the Semitic categories generally lost out and gave way to thinking in terms of such philosophical thought forms as: natures, essences, hypostases, *prosopa, idiomata*, generation, and procession. Christian Orthodoxy defined Jesus as the Son of God whose being is on the same level as the Father's. It is hardly surprising that when Christians in later centuries encountered early Jewish Christian views of Jesus in the Qur'an, they were quick to dub Islam a "Christian heresy." The conflict in the ancient church between a "low" and a "high" Christology is thus continued today in the Christian-Muslim dialogue.

There are other aspects of Christology that come into focus. Strangely, some passages in the Qur'an seem to deny that Jesus died on the cross. It is strange because the Qur'an generally admits that the fate of the prophets was to be killed. And yet Jesus is an exception. Why? There is no explanation. Some scholars think that this is due to the docetist influence of some heretical Christian sect. The Elkesaites, for instance, denied that Jesus died—in being God he must be immortal. If he did die, his death is at best the culmination of a life of obedience, self-sacrifice, and submission to the will of God. Nothing in the Qur'an speaks of the atoning death of Jesus. The teaching on the resurrection is equally ambiguous. The Qur'an speaks sometimes of Jesus' resurrection from the dead and sometimes of Jesus' assumption and ascension. In any case, for Muslims Jesus is not dead; he was taken up body, soul, and spirit, and is alive with God in the glory of heaven.

Hinduism. The image of Jesus has made an impact on modern Hinduism. Raja Ram Mohan Roy (1773-1833 C.E.) became convinced that India needed an ethical revival and that the best resource for this could be found in the Sermon on the Mount. Radhakrishnan and Gandhi were equally impressed with the teachings of the historical Jesus. His significance for them, however, was not in his concrete historical person but in the eternal word and wisdom which he exemplified in his life and teachings. Gandhi, who often read the Sermon on the Mount, praised Jesus for his exemplary life and his willingness to suffer and die for the truth.

Gandhi remarked: "The message of Jesus, as I understand it, is contained in his Sermon on the Mount. The spirit of the Sermon on the Mount competes with the Bhagavadgita, on fairly equal terms, for the mastery of my heart. It is this Sermon that endeared Jesus to me."[19] And this is what Gandhi had to say about Jesus' example of nonviolence and his way to the cross:

> Although I cannot claim to be a Christian in a confessional sense, still the example of Jesus' suffering is a factor in the make-up of my fundamental belief in non-violence that guides all my worldly

> and temporal actions. Jesus would have lived in vain and died in vain, if he did not teach us to direct our lives according to the eternal law of love.[20]

There is a certain ambivalence in the Hindu response to the biblical-Christian proclamation of Jesus Christ. One side would stress the concrete historical Jesus, his life and teachings, the Sermon on the Mount and his way to the cross, believing that this is the challenge that India needs the most. The image of Jesus the liberator in down-to-earth terms is most attractive. The revolutionary love of Jesus can motivate people to meet the needs of the poor and the oppressed. Another side would stress the mythical Christ that enshrines the nameless and utterly transcendent Reality itself. In this view Christ stands for the center of reality that has many names. Jesus is but one name alongside others such as Krishna, Rama, Isvara, and Purusha. This is Raimundo Panikkar's thesis in *The Unknown Christ of Hinduism*, which certainly fits the inclusive spirit of the Hindu religious traditions.

Hinduism can incorporate Christ and Christianity into its pluriform structure. It prides itself on its tolerance; it can accept all religions insofar as they lead people to perfection. All Hinduism asks is that Christianity give up all exclusive claims about Jesus Christ as the one and only Lord and Savior of humankind. The human Jesus may be fully accepted as a yogi or guru, as one among many. But the split between Jesus and Christ is maintained. The relation between the universal and the particular is conceived in terms of an ahistorical mystical pantheistic ontology. Jesus is simply one of many avatars, one of the many incarnations of the divine. As such Jesus is relegated to a secondary plane of being, not on the same level of Brahma. The questions that Christians would ask are: Which of the many incarnations truly represents ultimate reality? Which is definitive of final salvation? and Why is there need of another Savior than the One who has come, whose name is Jesus Christ?

Buddhism. Our discussion so far has concentrated on how other religious traditions view Jesus, pursuant to our proposal that Jesus Christ is the meeting ground of the religions in an age of universal history. We have not attempted to provide descriptions and comparisons of the basic structures and features of the various religions. Instead, we have asked how each of the religions tends to see Jesus in terms of its own worldview and system of salvation, with a view to finding some points of contact for the dialogue between the world religions.

Buddhists inevitably interpret Jesus and his message in light of their own understanding of Buddha and his teachings. Christians inevitably tend to draw comparisons and locate differences between Christ and Buddha. As Jesus is the Christ, the anointed One, so also Gautama is the Buddha, the enlightened One.

As Christians have had to distinguish between the Jesus of history and the later history of christological interpretations, Buddhists too are faced with the problem of distinguishing the authentic teachings of Buddha from subsequent revisions and developments. As Christians function with a christological canon of truth, judging religious and moral issues in light of the scriptural witness to Christ, so also the various Buddhist schools and movements appeal to the classic Buddhist texts which transmit the teachings and the spirit of the Buddha. Just as there is no consensus among Christian scholars concerning the historical Jesus, there is likewise no consensus among Eastern scholars on the real Gautama of history. However, the historical question has not proved to be so crucial in Buddhism as in Christianity. Some scholars go as far as to say that if the Buddha never existed as a historical figure, the truth of the Buddhist teachings would not change. However, Christianity would lose its gospel apart from the historical person of Jesus. Yet, most scholars are not so imbued with skepticism as to doubt the key features of Gautama's life and teachings.

Buddhists see many similarities between the story of Gautama and the story of Jesus. Although Gautama came from a background of wealth, and Jesus didn't, both became poor wandering preachers with a message of salvation. Both gathered disciples and taught them in the everyday language of the people, using stories, parables, and proverbs. Both were critical of the religious authorities, the scribes and the priests, and entered into conflict with them. Both demanded of people a radical change of heart and direction, a total commitment, not halfway measures. Both saw that people are afflicted by a tendency to care too much for the things of this passing world, to absolutize things that are purely relative.

Both Buddhism and Christianity emphasize an inordinate drive in humans to put themselves first, call it selfishness, greed, or egoism. Buddhism solves this problem by denying any reality to the self. Christianity, on the other hand, stresses liberating the self for other-centered love and behavior.

There are additional decisive differences between Buddhism and Christianity. The heart of Buddhist faith is the Four Noble Truths that Buddha preached following his enlightenment. They are: life is suffering; suffering has a cause; there is release from suffering; and there is a way of release. There is nothing like this in Jesus' teaching. For Jesus the world was created by God and is therefore good. There is suffering in the world, but life is not inherently suffering. The solution to the problem of suffering was not to withdraw from its toils and troubles. Jesus came from a Hebrew world of thought, that thinks in terms of a beginning and an end of the world, of history moving toward a future goal; Gautama came from the Hindu world of thought with its law of karma, innumerable reincarnations and world cycles. The difference brings out the contrast between the mystical spirit of Eastern religions and the prophetic spirit of the Hebraic tradition, linking Judaism, Christianity, and Islam. The mystical spirit tends to withdraw from the world and turn inward, counting on meditation to bring about detachment and finally enlightenment. The prophetic spirit answers the call of the kingdom to change the world, to care for others, to struggle for peace and justice, and to conform this world to God's will.

The sharpest way to depict this contrast is to compare the smiling Buddha sitting on a lotus blossom to the twisted figure hanging on the cross. The symbol of Buddha stands for inner tranquillity, peace, harmony, and good humor, the result of entering nirvana already in this life. The symbol of the crucified Christ stands for rejection, failure, agony, and dereliction, the result of the supreme sacrifice of love. Is there anything in Buddhism that can anticipate the cross as the ultimate disclosure of life's meaning, destiny, and salvation? Here, too, as in the case of the other religions, it seems that the cross is the rock of offense that sets the gospel in sharp contrast to the spiritual wisdom with which the great religions are so richly endowed.

SALVATION THROUGH CHRIST ALONE

If Jesus of Nazareth, whom Christians believe to be the Savior of the world, becomes the focal point of interreligious dialogues on a global scale, all will find themselves confronted by an enigmatic figure. Mark, the earliest Gospel, is shot through with a variety of questions about Jesus' true identity:

- *Mark 1:27*—And they were all amazed, so that they questioned among themselves, saying, "What is this? A new teaching! With authority he commands even the unclean spirits, and they obey him."
- *Mark 2:7*—"Why does this man speak thus? It is blasphemy! Who can forgive sins but God alone?"
- *Mark 4:41*—And they were filled with awe, and said to one another, "Who then is this, that even wind and sea obey him?"
- *Mark 8:27, 29*—And Jesus went on with his disciples, to the villages of Caesarea Philippi; and on the way he asked his disciples, "Who do men say that I am?" . . . And he asked them, "But who do you say that I am?"
- *Mark 14:61*—But he was silent and made no answer. Again the high priest asked him, "Are you the Christ, the Son of the Blessed?"

These questions are samples of the great christological ferment in early Christianity. There is an equally great ferment in our time. Many people are not satisfied with the old traditional formulations, but they cannot escape the original questions. The twentieth century is still grappling with the question, "Who do you say that I am?" The core of the classical Christian answers to this question contains the belief that Jesus is Savior, the Savior of Jews and Gentiles, creating a "third race" of people called out of all the nations and gathered together in a new community. This new community, called the church, was commissioned by the risen Christ in these words:

> Go therefore and make disciples of all nations, baptizing them in the name of the Father and of the Son and of the Holy Spirit,

teaching them to observe all that I have commanded you; and lo, I am with you always, to the close of the age. (Matt. 28:19-20)

The presupposition of the church's positive response to this command is the conviction that all people are in need of the gospel of God's salvation in Jesus Christ. But what is salvation? The Bible contains a multiplicity of words and images to depict the reality of salvation, such as: redemption, reconciliation, justification, sanctification, and atonement. These words and images are attempts to picture the saving work which Jesus accomplished through his life, ministry, death, and resurrection. This saving work constitutes God's "good news" which Christian believers are asked to broadcast to all human beings, on the supposition that they need to hear it. Paul says: "But how are men to call upon him in whom they have not believed? And how are they to believe in him of whom they have never heard? And how are they to hear without a preacher?" (Rom. 10:14). The message to be preached, heard, and believed is the good news that the New Testament teaches is absolutely unique, universal, decisive, and definitive of salvation for all humanity and the world.

Salvation: Our Need and Its Meaning

The Christian dialogue about Jesus the Christ with people of other faiths will necessarily include a grappling with the meaning of salvation and the different ways in which they claim to experience it. The Christian view of salvation moves between two poles of understanding. The first pole is the universal human need of salvation; the second is the appearance of the Savior in history.

Let us consider the first pole—the universal need of salvation. There is no single symbol to depict it. There are many ways to symbolize the lack in the human condition which salvation is supposed to meet, be it a state of bondage, disease, oppression, evil, darkness, nothingness, sin, or death. Common to all these images is a basic split in human existence, between the self in its present situation of need and the self in its future state of salvation. Every religion trades on such a split in the structure of being human in the world. The self is divided; one side exists here and now with all its needs and lacks; the other side will exist, if the religion in question delivers what it promises, in a state of fullness and satisfaction, even if such a state should be pictured as transcending the concrete self in a future nirvana. If there were no dualism in the human condition, if people were already whole, there would be no need for salvation. Religions would go out of business, as some prophets of the so-called secular age have prophesied—Comte, Marx, and Freud. In biblical symbolism, once the kingdom of God has fully arrived there will be no need for the temple, the church, or any kind of religion.

The world of the religions offers various symbols of that other dimension of reality which promises to be fully salvific—immortality, reincarnation, resurrection, metempsychosis, and the like. Some of these images picture the future of salvation as returning to "paradise lost." Others point forward to a future that has never been, whether a utopia here on earth or heavenly bliss above and beyond this world.The list of places of salvation is legion, including Olympus, Empyrium, Atlantis, Elysium, Valhalla, nirvana, and others like them.

The point is that the religions do not share a common view of ultimate salvation. For some the time of salvation lies in the past; for others it will come in the future. The feeling of nostalgia is appropriate to the primordial past, whereas passionate longing and expectation drive toward the future. We can see the logic of salvation at work in all the symbols and stories of salvation, no matter where it is located or when its time is due. The realm of salvation may be somewhere in space and time, here and now, though hidden from ordinary eyes, or it may lie above and beyond this world of time and history. Whatever the case may be, salvation thinking negates the negatives in present experience and anticipates a superlative transcendence in another dimension of reality.

At the present time there is no consensus among scholars on what constitutes real salvation. There is no underlying common idea of salvation that is mediated by the various religions. Buddhists and Hindus and Muslims and Jews and Christians do not experience the same salvation through their stories and symbols and sacraments. Even within the Judeo-Christian tradition there are different conceptions about the nature and meaning of salvation. Since the period of the Enlightenment, a shift has taken place in the way salvation is symbolized. Images of salvation that picture a supernatural realm in which heavenly bliss and happiness will reign forever seem to have lost much of their persuasive power. Many of our contemporaries seem to hold out hope within the limits of this world alone. The term "secular humanism" has been coined to refer to such a purely this-worldly view of the human project. Salvation—if the word is even used at all—is something that humans will work out through their own planning and praxis. The major factor in this "paradigm shift" is the change from a God-centered hope of salvation to a humanistic focus on personal happiness and social welfare. Revolutionary Marxism is the most conspicuous example of a movement that declares itself atheistic while counting on human beings to bring about a future paradise on earth, free of poverty, hunger, injustice, and exploitation. The biblical symbols of the reign of God and eternal life have been transformed into a utopian vision of peace and harmony in a classless society.

It is difficult to take the full measure of the impact of science and technology on traditional views of salvation. Each religion is being confronted by the challenge of modernity and is hard pressed to articulate the meaning of salvation under the conditions of the new universal culture emerging around the world. Traditional images of salvation are necessarily affected by a shift from superhuman to human power, from trust in the power of Providence to belief in salvation based on human potentiality.

Concurrent with this optimistic estimate of the human potential to build the socio-historical equivalent of the kingdom of God on earth, there seems to be growing a pervasive pessimism about the human project. Existentialist and nihilistic philosophers have expressed this feeling in terms of the "meaninglessness of human existence." Traditional religious images of salvation are being renewed as people have second thoughts about placing the hope of salvation entirely in human hands without the help of God. At first the humanistic approach seemed to endow human beings with greater dignity, by taking over operations which the religions had placed in the hands of God. There is, however, much evidence from the twentieth century that humans are botching the job of being God to themselves. With the obligation to produce their own salvation, people are becoming afflicted with doubt and despair, which in turn raises questions about the worthwhileness of life itself. By means of science and technology, the human race has used its power to create the means to blow itself off the face of the earth. There is a sick feeling at the core of existence, a loss of hope for this world, and a failure of courage. If God is dead, not only is heaven bare but the world becomes an increasingly lonely and dangerous place to exist.

These reflections lead to the conclusion that the attempt to define human salvation apart from the power of God, within the limits of this world alone, has proved to be a failure. The depth of the religious question about salvation cannot be reached within the framework of the post-Enlightenment worldview controlled by scientific humanism, a view which reduces our understanding of reason and nature, justice and peace, progress and development to the level of worldly existence. The Christian understanding of salvation contains dimensions of meaning that transcend the limits of a radically immanentistic worldview. Its questions and answers move in a wider orbit in which the reality and truth of the absolute transcendence of God are taken as given presuppositions.

Jesus the Savior

Even so, there is no single model of salvation in the biblical-Christian tradition. The spectrum of salvation images is very wide, and various of them have had a long history in the preaching and worship of the church. As the Swedish theologian, Gustaf Aulen, has shown in his book *Christus Victor*, there are different motifs around which the interpretations of the person and work of Christ have clustered over the centuries. In one motif Jesus is portrayed as the Victor over sin, death, and the devil; in another Jesus is presented as the sacrificial Victim; in still another Jesus is remembered as an Exemplar modeling the moral life.

The important point, however, is that all of them spell out salvation as an interpretation of the story of Jesus of Nazareth, his birth, his life and teachings, his death and resurrection, and his continuing influence in the power of the Spirit in the church and the world.

What images or motifs shall we use today to express the saving meaning of Jesus Christ? The meaning of salvation is multidimensional. No one theory of redemption can cover the meaning of Jesus Christ for all times and places. The contextual character of faith and theology requires that talk about salvation should reflect all sorts of needs and conditions, as well as both personal and communal dimensions of experience before God and in the world. The ancient church represented Jesus to the Hellenistic world as the Logos, since the Logos was an important concept in Greek philosophical thought. In the medieval period Jesus was pictured as one who restored the divinely created order of life that had been broken by sin, using metaphors based on the feudal order. In modern times Jesus becomes the liberator who pioneers the history of freedom as the answer to the quest for human fulfillment.

Today a number of theologians are reworking Luther's theology of the cross to interpret the suffering and death of Jesus commensurate with the tragic experiences of the twentieth century—two world wars, Auschwitz, nuclear holocaust, the gulags, Vietnam, mass starvation, AIDS, and a myriad of other forms of evil. The simple expression, "Jesus died for us," gives rise to reflection on God's participation in the suffering and death of every person through Jesus, who is God's representative. But Jesus is also the representative of humanity before God. His representative role functions in both directions, from God to humanity and from humanity to God. Luther spoke of this mediatory role as "the happy exchange." The cross of Jesus was an act by which God represented his participation in human suffering. As Dietrich Bonhoeffer said, "Only a suffering God can help."[21] Whole theologies are being written from the perspective of "the crucified God," most notably those by Jürgen Moltmann, Eberhard Jüngel, and Douglas John Hall. Although we cannot explicate this kind of theology in full, we refer to it as an example of how each age interprets the story of Jesus of Nazareth in light of its own struggles and experiences of life.

We have shown that there is a plurality of images of salvation that are relative to the context in which they are used. But Christians believe there is only one absolute Savior of the world. Acts 4:12 states it most clearly: "And there is salvation in no one else, for there is no other name under heaven given among men by which we must be saved." The New Testament abounds with titles of honor which identify the uniqueness of Jesus. We cannot subtract these titles from the New Testament picture of Jesus of Nazareth and have any real resemblance of the man Jesus. Our dialogue with people of other faiths may begin with this or that aspect of the picture of Jesus, but in the last analysis we will want to take a good look at the whole biblical picture of Jesus as the Christ, or as the Son of God, Logos, Lord, and Savior. All of these titles served to elevate the person of Jesus to the place of majesty and glory which Israel had reserved for the One God, so much so that Jewish monotheism gave way to Christian trinitarianism. Judging from the history of Christianity, persistent inquiry into the identity and meaning of Jesus paved the way for redefining the nature of God in terms of the doctrine of the Trinity, One God in the three persons of Father, Son, and Holy Spirit.

The doctrine of the Trinity frames not only the uniqueness of Jesus but also his universality. Because of Jesus' special relation to God, Jesus is unique; because of God's special relation to Jesus, Jesus has universal meaning. His unique identity and his universal meaning belong together—two sides of the same coin. The concrete person, Jesus of Nazareth, is unique because of his unsurpassable universal significance. Because of the uniqueness and universality of Jesus, there is a large hope of salvation, not only for those few who already believe, but also for the many who do not yet believe in the gospel. The mission of the community of faith in world history is shaped by this tension between the "already" and the "not yet" of faith in Jesus as Savior. It is clearly God's announced will that all people shall be saved and come to the knowledge of truth (1 Tim. 2:4).

Meanwhile we live in a global situation in which the gospel of salvation in Jesus' name is still a matter of dispute. Is this gospel really true? Can those who believe in Jesus Christ expect to convince others of their need of his saving benefits? There are billions of people who do not know or believe in Jesus. At the same time, millions are prepared to confess him and bear witness that God was in Christ working out the world's salvation. There is a paradox here; with Paul we might speak of a "mystery." God's will to save all is believed by only a few. This fact has driven theologians to speculate about the ultimate resolution of this paradox in God's eternity. Neither dialogues nor speculations will resolve the mystery of salvation. Meanwhile we can live by hope and offer a prayer that God will deal with the world and every person according to God's gracious word in Jesus Christ.

In the Christian dialogue with people of other faiths, we will also hear their testimonies concerning their experience of salvation. For example, from Buddhists we will hear about illumination, from Hindus about unification, from Marxists about revolutionary transformation, from Muslims about submission to the will of Allah. We can then compare these concepts with what Christians mean by the forgiveness of sins, overcoming estrangement with God, or resurrection unto new life beyond death. But the popular view that all religions provide the same salvation, only by different means, does not mesh with the experience of people who have converted from one faith to another. Buddhists or Hindus who convert to the Christian faith do not usually speak of sameness but of difference. For Christians the normative meaning of salvation lies in the gospel of God's reconciling work in Jesus Christ.

Those who stand within the Reformation tradition have placed a strong emphasis on the sole mediatorship of Jesus Christ. The righteousness of God and the justification of the sinful world are communicated on account of Christ alone and received through faith alone. The doctrine of justification by grace alone through faith alone on account of Christ alone has been called the "article by which the church stands or falls." The basis and center of this article is the gospel of Christ, in whom the love of God has broken through the barriers of human sinfulness and

God's wrath. It is the overwhelming power of God's love that drives Christians to meet all others in the sure confidence that this love is wide enough to be all-inclusive, uniting all those who are now separated in the eternal circle of God's mercy.

NOTES

1. Jaroslav Pelikan, *Jesus Through the Centuries* (New Haven: Yale University Press, 1985) (Hereafter cited as *Jesus*).
2. Albert Schweitzer, *The Quest of the Historical Jesus* (London: Adam & Charles Black, 1910), 4 (Hereafter cited as *The Quest*).
3. Pelikan, *Jesus*, 220.
4. Schweitzer, *The Quest*, 3.
5. Dietrich Bonhoeffer, *Letters and Papers from Prison*, edited by Eberhard Bethge (New York: The Macmillan Company, 1972), 278-82 (Hereafter cited as *Letters*).
6. Paul Tillich, *Systematic Theology* (Chicago: The University of Chicago Press, 1957), 2: 150.
7. This is the point made by Martin Kahler in *The So-Called Historical Jesus and the Historic Biblical Christ*, trans., ed., and intro. Carl E. Braaten (Philadelphia: Fortress Press, 1964).
8. Edward Schillebeeckx, *Jesus—An Experiment in Christology*, trans. Hubert Hoskins (New York: The Seabury Press, 1979).
9. E. P. Sanders, *Jesus and Judaism* (Philadelphia: Fortress Press, 1985).
10. Hans Küng & Pinchas Lapide, *Jesus im Widerstreit, Ein judischchristlicher dialog* (Stuttgart: Calwer Verlag, 1981), 43.
11. For a more detailed treatment of the origin and development of Christology in the early church, see my essay titled, "The Person of Jesus Christ," in *Christian Dogmatics*, ed. Carl E. Braaten and Robert W. Jenson (Philadelphia: Fortress Press, 1984), 1: 465-569.
12. Karl Barth, *Church Dogmatics*, trans. G. W. Bromiley (Edinburgh: T & T. Clark, 1961), IV/3: 114.
13. Ibid., 115.
14. Elisabeth Schussler Fiorenza, *In Memory of Her* (New York: Crossroads, 1983).
15. Robert Hammerton-Kelly, *God the Father* (Philadelphia: Fortress Press, 1979).
16. Pinchas Lapide, *Israelis, Jews, and Jesus*, trans. Peter Heinegg (Garden City, N.Y.: Doubleday & Co., 1979), 81.
17. Ibid., 31-32.
18. Franz Rosenzweig, *The Star of Redemption*, trans. William W. Hallo from the second edition of 1930 (New York: Holt, Rinehart and Winston, 1970).
19. Quoted by Hans Küng, *Christianity and World Religions*, trans. Peter Heinegg (Garden City, N.Y.: Doubleday & Co., 1986), 282.
20. Ibid.
21. Bonhoeffer, *Letters*, 220.

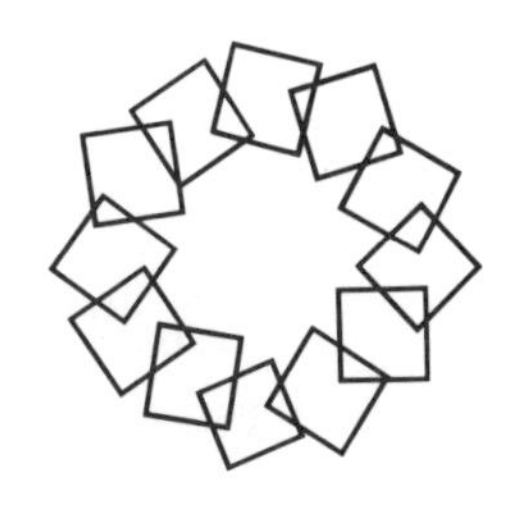

4

THE TRUTH WILL MAKE YOU FREE

Paul R. Sponheim

> Jesus then said to the Jews who had believed in him, "If you continue in my word, you are truly my disciples, and you will know the truth, and the truth will make you free" (John 8:31-32).

IS THE CHRISTIAN FAITH TRUE?

The Christian faith claims to describe truly what is real. Does it? Carl Braaten has stressed the Christian's "sure confidence" in the universal and unconditional love of God in Christ. With stakes that high, it is important to consider the nature and basis of the Christian's confidence. Is the word of Jesus about the truth itself true? The answer matters. It matters because the Christian faith claims to be true. The faith makes claims about what is real. This seems so obvious that it is almost unnecessary to say so. But it is necessary because the truth claim, though essential to faith, is not often faced squarely.

Importance of the Question

To recognize that the Christian faith claims to be true is not a trivial exercise in understanding that faith. One is not done with the analysis of Christian faith even when one mentions so important a matter as that this faith entails trust in a personal God. Yes, such trust is important, but it is not formless or contentless. Speaking of an appropriate attitude or disposition does not exhaust the meaning of faith. The Christian makes a claim about what is really the case about history, humankind, nature, the future—about God. Faith claims knowledge. Thus Martin Luther believed he was arguing about the nature of reality when he was in dispute with Erasmus. He cried, "Take away assertions and you take away Christianity."[1] Luther was right. The Christian faith collapses in self-contradiction or in hopeless category confusion, if one denies that truth claims are being made in this faith. The creeds and confessions of Christendom, its educational efforts within and its missionary activities without, its colleges and seminaries—and its congregations among its churches—clearly all these are not mustered to regulate a set of behaviors or to massage a mood without regard to what is real for and beyond the believer.

Order and Meaning Are Grounded in the Creative Word

In its self-understanding Christian faith traces this matter of truth all the way back to its source. The church takes its life from the Word of God, the Word which is the ground of meaning. The opening sentence of John's Gospel expresses the Christian view of things: "In the beginning was the Word, and the Word was with God, and the Word was God" (John 1:1). Within the very life of God, before and apart from the human struggle for meaning, there was the word, there was truth.[2] And because God is a speaking God, there came to be a world. Because God is Word, that which was made by God was a cosmos, an ordered whole. The world was and is held together by the Word of God. It was that Word that came in human flesh for our salvation. When that salvation is complete, we will know as we are known, face to face. Between alpha and omega lies the aching reality of the agony and ecstasy of history. And there stands the cross of God of which Braaten has written so emphatically in the preceding chapter. That cross is itself a testimony to God's claim on history. And thus a theology "of the cross" is called to face reality fully.

In the twenty-first of the Heidelberg theses, Martin Luther wrote, "A theology of glory calls evil good and good evil. A theology of the cross calls the thing what it actually is."[3]

Thus the claim that the Christian faith makes truth claims is not an interpretation imposed on the faith. The faith is a faith *in* God. It is also a faith *that* God: that God is the maker of this universe, that God acted in history to save all, that God will judge the living and the dead. Trust and belief are welded together in faith. Faith trusts a God who is known through self-revelation. This is a God who speaks to create and to save. And the word of this God stands. God is a God who makes and keeps covenants with people. "If we are faithless, he remains faithful—for he cannot deny himself" (2 Tim. 2:13).

Meaning Is Essential to Salvation

The truth question matters to us for, as humans, meaning is essential to our salvation. Thus the truth question matters to the Christian. It matters that the Christian faith is claiming to be true. It matters that the truth question be asked and that it be answered. It matters to us as well simply as human beings. We will not be saved—healed, fulfilled, brought to flower—without the truth.

It may be too exclusive to say with A. N. Whitehead that when God created humankind, God created language.[4] But whatever is said about communication among dolphins, when we set about to understand the nature of human beings we must speak of human language. Through language, we are creatures who can move beyond a stimulus-response bondage to our environment. By signs and symbols we find and shape a world in which we can dream, anticipate, plan, relate, and act. Socrates was right: An unexamined life is not worth living. We are questioning beings who rise above immediate concerns with survival to ask for meanings: Why? Why not? How? As humans, the truth question matters to us.

Is the Christian Faith Too Good to Be True?

In principle the Christian faith fits the human condition. At least, the fit is there formally. We are looking for meaning; the Christian faith offers a message which seems to fulfill that quest. Several questions arise when we ask whether the Christian news is actually good for human beings. Clearly, human quest and gospel gift do not make a perfect marriage without toil and pain. The Christian understands this. The Christian may speak here of the dark and darkening reality of sin. Often we do not know what we are looking for and we are looking in the wrong place. And even when we find the gospel or are found by it, questions remain. The claim of Christian faith to be true is just that, a claim. It places before the questing human person the next question: Is it true?

St. John writes that grace and truth came through Jesus Christ. Perhaps there is a sort of grace about any truth. Meaning is a meeting; the one who comes to know is one who is received in a relationship. In this there is at least the grace of order. But beyond this there is the question whether the content of the word received is itself good news. And so there is the question whether the Christian claim about truth and grace is itself true. Freud is not the only one to ask whether the very goodness of the news should not arouse suspicion. Is this news too good to be true? Does it suggest the power of wish-fulfillment?[5] The Christian should gladly accept Freud's question, for it is a good one. It does matter whether the word of grace is true. It claims to be true. We are looking for truth and we must not settle for grace without truth, for sentimentality without substance. The faith accepts the challenge. This word, it believes, will not return void.

The Reality of Pluralism

The truth question matters as we approach the reality of pluralism. It is commonplace to speak of this time as a pluralistic age. That means we need to focus on the fact that other faiths are an undeniable part of our context. The truth question matters because we are living in a time when it is particularly difficult and particularly important to deal with this question.

In 1986, in responding to a formal Lutheran Church in America request, the Lutheran Council in the USA issued some "guidelines on inter-faith worship." However, we are talking about more than Lutherans and Presbyterians at this point! Today's concern with pluralism involves all world faiths. This concern, of course, is the occasion for this book. The reality of pluralism emphasizes some key problems.

To claim all these mutually exclusive faiths are true is to give up the truth question. How does this pluralism connect with our concern with the truth status of the Christian faith? Several alternatives seem to be available. Perhaps the one that is most readily available is simply to acknowledge the claims of all the faiths. This approach, which seems very popular, amounts to giving up the truth claim of the Christian faith. After all, what is clear about other faiths is that they are indeed plural and other. The study of parallels and continuities is important, of course. But even theologians who eagerly seek such common ground in dialogue do need to admit that the faiths are not one. Thus John Cobb writes, "What is supremely important to the Buddhist is not what appears supremely important to the Christian. "Christ" and "Buddha" do not name the same reality."[6] Cobb could have gone on to cite such fundamental differences as those depending on the very existence of God. Given this stubborn otherness or plurality, it becomes difficult to suppose that somehow they all speak of God. We want to say that God is one, but we need to grant that the faiths are plural. Their plurality hardly suggests a witness to the divine unity.

In what sense could contradictory claims be true? If they all cannot be true, why not be evenhanded and regard them all as false? It is tempting to settle for saying that these human claims to know God (or to know transcendence without God) are just that, human. It is tempting to say that they are that and only that, "truly" significant expressions of human sensibility. Or, better, to say they are neither true nor false. They are appealing varieties for our spiritual taste buds, but not rival representations of reality.

This tendency to read the given text of pluralism through such relativistic glasses is strongly supported by another aspect of our current consciousness. At an earlier time in this century, the appeal to proof by the senses provided a challenge to the church. "If your God is real," the skeptic said, "then show me the evidence hard and fast, just as I can, for what we recognize to be real in the world." Christians were wise not to accept the terms of that challenge, though some may have tended to drive into the opposite ditches of either the sheer inwardness of faith or the absolute futurity of Christian truth.

Now the challenge is different. Several voices seem to be denying that any of the self's statements can refer significantly to a world beyond the self. Thomas Kuhn in science, Richard Rorty in philosophy, and Humberto Maturana in family therapy—to name only a few prominent examples—represent such a tendency to collapse the world back into the self.[7] If even the scientist's knowing is stuck in subjectivity, surely it seems the more likely that we should not try to arbitrate the conflicting claims in so personal a realm as religion!

These two impulses—the religious call to embrace all the faiths as knowing "the many names of God"[8] and the secular suggestion that in knowing we know only ourselves (the first a more "objective" relativism, the second a more "subjective" one)—seem to keep company with a moral appeal to complete openness in interreligious conversation. It is as if a vacuum is supposed to be the best conversation partner. In such a case the conversation does indeed bid to become vacuous. In their dialogues, Lutherans and Roman Catholics would not do well to meet saying, "I don't believe anything; you don't believe anything . . . Let's talk." For the kind of conversation in which truth is well sought, identity and integrity are needed. Because I am someone—a Christian—I can truly meet someone else. In the give and take of this meeting, truth can be served concretely.

To claim only Christian faith is true is to deny that faith's universal vision. Of course, other responses to pluralism are possible. Facing the dizzying plethora of religious options and recalling the unity of God, the Christian may be tempted not only to consider but also to close the truth question. Why not let the "no other name by which we must be saved" motif minister to us the healing balm that only Christianity has truth?

Clearly there are difficulties with this response. On the word of the Christian gospel itself, God would have all to be saved (1 Tim. 2:4). Suppose we say that Christianity and the other religions are rivals and then single out Christianity as humankind's proper suitor. Have we solved a problem or created one? We can say we have the one real God. But is it not problematic that the Christian God, the true God, has no more than a minority following after all these centuries? We are told that God wants all. But is not this God strangely ineffective? Ironically, thus to protect the uniqueness of the Christian God seems to be undercut the very credentials of that God. Moreover, the Christian text itself refuses the simplification involved in this response, for it speaks of God's witness and word well beyond the boundaries of Christendom: God has not left any people without some witness (Acts 14:17). Thus, given the actual plurality of faiths and given the Christian faith's own claim on the others, simply to say only Christianity is true is not to engage the truth question adequately.

The truth question is engaged as we seek to find the truth in the genuine interaction (mutual witness) of the faiths. Happily, another response is possible. It is possible to address the truth question precisely in the pluralistic setting. Perhaps all the religions do not ask the truth question in the same way. From the Christian's vantage point, however, these faiths do compete in trying to offer some gospel to the human quest for salvific meaning. So the question of truth is not imposed on this context. It can be asked and it must be asked.

Carl Braaten has proposed that the question be asked and answered in terms of the "rock of offense," the place that Jesus holds in God's history with the world. Braaten knows, of course, that these faiths will not be content merely to ask the question quietly and then take their seats while the Christian faith takes the pulpit to answer in monologic arrogance. It matters that the truth question be asked and answered precisely in the context of the faiths, of which Christianity is but one. Braaten himself has put the matter this way:

> The gospel does not meet the world religions on a one-way street, giving them the traditional symbols of Christology and receiving

> nothing back. The dialogue will be a two-way street, in which the condition of openness to the other religions will be motivated by knowledge that they also somehow speak of Jesus Christ. . . . For God is not without witnesses in these religions.[9]

It matters that, together, we ask and answer the question of truth.

HOW DO WE KNOW THE TRUTH?

Very well, let us suppose it does matter that the question of the truth of the Christian faith be asked and answered. Since it matters, we do well to consider what one might fairly expect of any answer. We are speaking about human beings claiming to know God. What would do as an adequate answer will have to do with the human and with God. We need to ask how it is that humans know. And we need to ask how God, such a one as the Christian believes God to be, could be known. In doing this we do not answer the question of God, but we clarify the conditions under which an appropriate answer could be considered.

Test of Coherence

If the Christian claim is true, it must not collapse in contradiction. The claim must be coherent. Trial attorneys cross-examine witnesses to find contradictions that could discredit their professed truthful testimonies. So the Christian claim must verily be a word, an utterance which is not merely a noise or a sound but has a meaning. And so the word must stand; it must not be cancelled out by a later word. The Christian faith accepts this test of coherence, for it believes that God is one and that God does not act or speak against God. Whether the Christian faith *passes* the test, of course, is a separate question.

This test does not mean that meaning is static. There may well be development, or even surprise. But without consistent continuity of meaning an utterance's candidacy for truth collapses. We perhaps do not expect language that emerges in interpersonal relationships to have the same kind of stability as a telephone directory (though we do want to have the *current* directory!). That will make a difference when we think about what the test of coherence requires of God language. Still, coherence remains a necessary test for truth claims.

Test of Correspondence

Coherence alone is not a sufficient test. While this age features tendencies to regard coherence as the sole test for truth, we must not abandon the stubborn commonsense understanding that a statement is true because it corresponds to reality. The human quest for meaning would be frustrated if we were all locked with the playing rules of our several tribal or individual language games. Of course, our language systems affect how we perceive reality. But language systems are first and finally in debt to reality. That is why persons can come to change their truth claims in really fundamental ways; we call it conversion.

The Christian faith agrees. Christian claims are understood to refer to something beyond themselves, ultimately to God. We need therefore a test of correspondence. This correspondence test is accepted by a faith believing God is real outside the believer and that God is known in the world. The words in the liturgical order of service do not depend for their weight upon their aesthetic elegance. The sentences in the dogmatics do not derive their importance from the intricacy of their internal relations. Christian claims matter because they claim to refer to God, who is understood to be real before and apart from the claiming. Moreover, in referring to God these claims also refer to something else beyond themselves—to the world. Earlier it was said that on the Christian view there is no world without the word. But now it must be said that on the same view there is no Word of God *for us* without the world. The world is where we live and where God meets us.

The word of God does not take us to heaven but to earth, the scene of God's creative redemptive and sanctifying activity. The World Council of Churches is thus right in claiming that "the very nature and content of our Christian confession draws Christians to pay the closest attention to the realities of the world as it has developed under God's creative, disciplinary and redemptive rule."[10] Dietrich Bonhoeffer put the point even more strongly:

> The reality of God discloses itself only by setting me entirely in the reality of the world and when I encounter the reality of the world, it is always already sustained, accepted and reconciled in the reality of God. . . . I never experience the reality of God without the reality of the world or the reality of the world without the reality of God.[11]

But is this true? Do we not experience the reality of the world without the reality of God? And as for experiencing the reality of God without the reality of the world, it is one thing for the Christian faith to accept the test of correspondence and quite another to pass it. But that all the world is involved in passing that test is well suggested by Wolfhart Pannenberg:

> The question about the truth of the Christian message has to do with whether it can still disclose to us today the unity of the reality in which we live, as it once did in the ancient world which was the basis for the victory of Christianity in the ancient *oikumene* surrounding the Mediterranean Sea. Thus, the questions regarding the truth of the Christian faith are not concerned with a particular truth of one kind or another but with truth itself, which in essence can only be one. It asks whether the Christian faith still contains the truth that gathers together everything experienced as real.[12]

Test of Power for the Future

When we have spoken the truth as coherence and as correspondence we are not done. We also need the test of power for the future which is accepted by a faith believing that full truth lies ahead. Therefore we are not done because neither word nor world is done. Perhaps that to which the word seeks to correspond should not be called a "world" after all. It is so clearly incomplete. Is that not also true of our life with word? Indeed, part of what will yet come to be will come to be precisely through the creative power of language.[13] Thus human reflection on truth talk leads to such "pragmatic" thinking as that of William James. "The truth of an idea is not a stagnant property inherent in it.

Truth *happens* to an idea. It *becomes* true, is *made* true by events. Its verity is in fact an event, a process; the process namely of its verifying itself, its veri-fication. Its validity is the process of its validation."[14]

Once again, the Christian faith can welcome this reference to what will be. Contemporary theologians as unlike as Karl Barth and Karl Rahner have recognized the bearing of this consciousness of temporality on our dogmatic claims. The Protestant Barth emphasized that the concrete dogmas of history point beyond themselves to the dogma which is the perfect knowledge of the word of God.[15] And his Roman Catholic counterpart, Rahner, recognized the essentially unfinished character of the work of dogmatic formulation:

> Once theologians and the ordinary magisterium of the Church have begun to pay attention to a reality and a truth revealed by God, the final result is always a precisely formulated statement. This is natural and inevitable. In no other way is it possible to mark the boundary of error and the misunderstanding of divine truth in such a way that this boundary will be observed in the day-to-day practice of religion. Yet while this formula is an end, an acquisition and a victory, which allows us to enjoy clarity and security as well as ease in instruction, if this victory is to be a true one the end must also be a beginning.[16]

Their counsel is appropriate. Jesus said the truth *will* make you free. Paul Varo Martinson has put the matter in this way:

> The question of truth is in the end an eschatological question; it is, so to say,open-ended towards the future, and has to do with final consequence. If the final consequence is that nothing matters—illogical though such a contradiction in terms might be—then that nothing matters is the truth that matters. If, however, something does in fact matter, then the question of truth—the truth about what matters—is a question that discloses the truth about me. We all, then, live at the point of eschatological risk.[17]

The knowing is recognized as human, involving the self-world distinction and a combination of ambiguity and certainty.

The Christian does not suppose that this openness of truth actually closes the process of testing. The future is being created even now; hence the Scriptures speak of the "first fruits" of Christian hope. We do not yet know as we will know, but we do know in part. Accordingly the Christian welcomes questions concerning the nature of the knowing involved in Christian claims. Bonhoeffer has already reminded us that Christian knowledge of God does not remove us from this world. This is true not only of what is known but of knowing itself. Martin Luther, commenting on Heb. 9:23, made this point in speaking about the hidden God. It is not that God cannot be known, but that God is to be known precisely through the ordinary:

> It is a great thing to be a Christian and to have one's life hidden, not in some place, as in the case of hermits, or in one's own heart, which is exceedingly deep, but in the invisible God himself, namely, to live amid the things of the world and to be nourished by what appears nowhere except by means of ordinary verbal indication and hearing alone.[18]

Christian truth claims well illustrate Luther's point. The Western world has tended to organize reality in the terms of the distinction between self and world. In our being and so in our knowing we are selves in the world. The church has followed that lead. Faith aside, knowing has been understood by way of the self (intuition, innate ideas, and the like) or by way of the world (sense perception, the knower as a blank page before experience). Similarly, Christians have followed two main lines in their knowing of God. Here is Paul Tillich's summary:

> One can distinguish two ways of approaching God: the way of overcoming estrangements and the way of meeting a stranger. In the first way, man discovers *himself* when he discovers God; he discovers something that is identical with himself although it transcends him infinitely, something from which he is estranged, but from which he never has been and never can be separated. In the second way man meets *a stranger* when he meets God. The meeting is accidental. Essentially they do not belong to each other. They may become friends on a tentative and conjectural basis. But there is no certainty about the stranger man has met. He may disappear, and only probable statements can be made about his nature.[19]

So once again the prospects seem encouraging, formally, for the Christian faith and the human critical quest for understanding to come together. At least the Christian faith does not propose to impose a whole new faculty of knowing. But this formal agreement puts before us a challenging agenda. Clearly, in linking itself with the human knowing process the Christian faith opens itself to the risks of that process. There is not only the possibility of error in what is claimed to be known. There is the risk of error in the knowing process itself. Perhaps the self-world distinction is not an indubitable structure at this point.[20] There is also the danger that we will operate with the view that there is only one truly human way to know. Happily, more recent studies of language and knowing increasingly recognize that one does not know the other who is a person just as one knows the other that is a machine.[21]

As one moves from machine to person, one's knowing encounters increasing ambiguity. Fortunately, there are voices emphasizing that such ambiguity does not amount to absurdity. Here is the testimony of a nontheist, Simone de Beauvoir, writing in the field of ethics:

> . . . the notion of ambiguity must not be confused with that of absurdity. To declare that existence is absurd is to deny that it can ever be given a meaning; to say that it is ambiguous is to assert that its meaning is never fixed, that it must be constantly won. Absurdity challenges every ethics; but also the finished rationalization of the real world leaves no room for ethics; it is because man's condition is ambiguous that he seeks, through failure and outrageousness, to save his existence.[22]

Christians are not the least needy when it comes to this warning. How shall one connect ambiguity of human knowing and the Christian knowing of God? There is the risk that we will see the second simply displacing the first. Daniel Taylor has summarized that kind of response:

> This desire for truth makes reflective Christians susceptible to a very widespread confusion in our culture—the confusion of *truth* with *certainty*. . . . Unfortunately, much of the church has also sold out to the myth of certainty. . . . "We don't have to float

> around like the poor secularist," we are told by the rationalistic Christian, "because we have absolutes. The secularist lost his absolute, our truth claims are certain, not contingent; objective, not subjective; eternal, not temporal."[23]

Perhaps there is a kind of certainty in faith. But it has to do more with the way in which a couple can be sure of each other after years of marriage than with that which can be objectified and measured. One needs to distinguish these two certainties.

Thus we have a more comprehensive approach to the question, "What would we do, it if were true?" And with that, we turn to the question itself.

IS THE CHRISTIAN FAITH TRUE?

Is the Christian claim itself coherent? Does it accurately refer to reality? Does it speak of that which will be true, and in speaking contribute to its power?

Coherence in the Focus on God Incarnate

In accepting the test of noncontradiction, the Christian faith relies on its confession that God is one. That point has already been made. It remains a question, however, whether what the Christian faith says of God actually hangs together. The Christian faith is challenged to find coherence in the focus on God incarnate, transcendence in relationship. Sadly, we must confess that in some of what we have said of God we have failed this test. Is it coherent to say that God is timeless and yet acts in time? Or that God cannot suffer but truly loves, and loves even unto death on a cross? We have surely strained the human sense of coherence in what we have said about the work of Christ. We have pitted Jesus against the God who sent him, dividing the blessed Trinity. Indeed, perhaps the greatest coherence problem with the Trinity is not the apparent arithmetic one, but the disjunctive ways in which we have spoken of the persons of God. The way some Christians are pitting God and Christ against each other is paralleled by other Christians who elevate the Holy Spirit—and, not so incidentally, exalt their possession of that Spirit—above and apart from the other persons of the Trinity.

We have confessions to make. But in doing so we should let our eyes be opened to see the unity from which we have strayed. The Bible is not a flatland of miscellaneous assertions. It is a story—we want to say a *true* story—of the gracious work of God in creation, judgment, and salvation. At their truest, Christian faith and theology focus on the unity found in this gracious God. The Christian cannot grant that this theme of unity has been preempted by any other world faith—for example Islam. Martin Luther understood that, even when probing the complexities of *The Bondage of the Will*:

> . . . the secret will of the Divine Majesty is not a matter for debate, and the human temerity which with continual perversity is always neglecting necessary things in its eagerness to probe this one, must be called off and restrained from busying itself with the investigation of these secrets of God's majesty, which is impossible to penetrate because he dwells in light inaccessible . . . Let it occupy itself instead with God incarnate, or as Paul puts it, with Jesus crucified, in whom are all the treasure of wisdom and knowledge, though in a hidden manner; for through him it is furnished abundantly with what it ought to know and ought not to know. It is God incarnate, moreover, who is speaking here: "I would . . . you would not"—God incarnate, I say, who has been sent into the world for the very purpose of willing, speaking, doing, suffering and offering to all men everything necessary for salvation.[24]

If Christian faith and theology follow Luther's admonition to center in the God "suffering and offering . . . everything necessary for salvation," the claim to coherence can be defended. There will be no need to offer God's commitment with one hand and take it back with the other, as if to protect God's transcendence while teasing the temporal with touches of immanence. The Christian faith recognizes that God has not stopped being God by becoming God for us. God's transcendence is precisely to be found in God's relationship to us, in God's commitment to us. This is nicely illustrated by Sören Kierkegaard. He speaks of a king who loved a humble maiden and *pretended* to be a servant boy in order to win the maiden's love. Love does seem to flourish between them. But then the king, tiring of this servant boy status, reveals the truth and bids the maiden join him in the palace. She is infuriated by the manipulation and deception of the king and all ends unhappily ever after. This kind of deception is not God's way says Kierkegaard. He explains:

> God's servant-form, however, is not a mere disguise, but is actual; it is not a parastatic body but an actual body; and from the hour that in the omnipotent purpose of his omnipotent love God became a servant, he has so to speak imprisoned himself in his resolve, and is now bound to go on (to speak foolishly) whether it pleases him or no. He cannot then betray himself. There exists for him no such possibility as that which is open to the noble king, suddenly to show that he is after all the king—which is no perfection in the king (that he has this possibility), but merely discloses his impotence, and the impotence of his resolve, that he cannot really become what he desires to be.[25]

The Christian church refuses to permit the God of the Old Testament to be pitted against the New Testament God. Rightly, for no other statement occurs as often in the Old Testament as this one:

> The Lord passed before him, and proclaimed, "The Lord, the Lord, a God merciful and gracious, slow to anger, and abounding in steadfast love and faithfulness, keeping steadfast love for thousands, forgiving iniquity and transgression and sin, but who will by no means clear the guilty (Exod. 34:6-7).[26]

This is not to deny that there is something new in the New Testament. The Old Testament, of course, looks precisely to this newness. And that which is new certainly has to do with the reality of human sin for God. Hosea reveals God's anguish:

> How can I give you up, O Ephraim!
>   How can I hand you over, O Israel?
> How can I make you like Admah!
>   How can I treat you like Zeboiim?
> My heart recoils within me,
>   my compassion grows warm and tender.
> I will not execute my fierce anger,
>   I will not again destroy Ephraim;
> For I am God and not man,

> the Holy One in your midst,
> and I will not come to destroy (Hos. 11:8-9).

God did come—so the Christian story has it, but not to destroy. And the Jesus who came does bear witness to the One who sent him. Consider the emphases Jesus makes in John's Gospel:

- I and the Father are one (10:30).
- The word which you hear is not mine,
  but the Father's who sent me (14:24).
- All that the Father has is mine (16:15).
- He who has seen me has seen the Father (14:9).

Similarly, the biblical teaching concerning the Holy Spirit is precisely about one who makes known the things of Christ. The Spirit "will not speak on his own authority," for he will take what is Christ's and declare it (John 16:13). There is no Christian reason to let these persons of God be driven apart in our thinking. One may distinguish, perhaps, among God "for us," "with us" and "in us," but one will speak of the one God.[27] The Christian church has recognized this unity dogmatically in emphasizing that the external works of God (creation, redemption, sanctification) are indivisible, while the inner works (begetting, breathing) divisibly reflect the inner and independent life of the Trinity.

The Christian need not fear the test of coherence. That seems clear. But the Christian theologian has work to do in meeting that test; that is also clear. Yet there is cause for optimism in "the faith delivered to the saints."

Correspondence in our God-talk

What of the second test? Do Christian claims truly correspond to reality outside themselves? The Christian faith is challenged to meet the correspondence test, to demonstrate that Christian God-talk connects with what we know apart from God. The God to be sought is not a God to be seen, as I have said. Accordingly, the question of correspondence becomes a matter not of proving that God is, or is a certain way, but of assessing whether Christian claims about God connect plausibly with reality as we know it most deeply and persistently. This is not begging the question, for faith does not define and designate the deep and the persistent. Indeed, if evil is a deep and persistent feature of what we know as real, God-claims must correspond with our experiences of evil.

God as ground and goal for self- and moral-directedness. Before we speak further of evil, we must first probe another question. Does the God-talk of Christian faith make sense in the light of what we know about self and world? First, what about the self? We recognize the self as a precarious project. We are caught up in the contingency of becoming, in which we seek the unity of equilibrium or continuity within change. An atheist who could see this project, while remaining pessimistic about its outcome, was J. P. Sartre:

> Every human reality is a passion in that it projects losing itself so as to found being and by the same stroke to constitute the In-itself which escapes contingency by being its own foundation, the *Ens Causa Sui* [that which is its own cause], which religions call God. Thus the passion of man is the reverse of that of Christ, for man loses himself as man in order that God may be born. But the idea of God is contradictory and we lose ourselves in vain. Man is a useless passion.[28]

The Christian faith connects with such nontheistic talk by speaking of God as both the ground and the goal of life. In its beginning and at its ending the self stands before God. In all its becoming, the self can know itself in relation to a constant and faithful God. Recall the words of the psalmist: "Whither shall I go from thy Spirit? . . . If I take the wings of the morning . . . thy hand shall lead me" (Ps. 139:7, 9-10).

God is not only "there" to ground the self in all its projects. God makes a claim on the self. The gift of life is also the task of life. The sense that life is directed, that it matters mightily how we conduct ourselves—this moral sense is manifestly not limited to theists. Perhaps this sense is keenest in the word of judgment. It matters what we choose; it matters—there will be an accounting. As Peter Berger put it in writing of "signals of transcendence," even for non-theists there are certain deeds which "cry out to heaven for judgment."[29] Christian faith need not speak anonymously of such judgment. The psalmist speaks clearly for humankind in seeking judgment. "Search me, O God, and know my heart! Try me and know my thoughts! And see if there by any wicked way in me. . . ." But the next line sounds a different tone: ". . . and lead me in the way everlasting!" (Ps. 139:23-24). And Paul the apostle celebrated the deed of judgment which answers that quest:

> What then shall we say to this? If God is for us, who is against us? He who did not spare his own Son but gave him up for us all, will he not also give us all things with him? Who shall bring any charge against God's elect? It is God who justifies; who is to condemn? Is it Christ Jesus, who died, yes, who was raised from the dead, who is at the right hand of God, who indeed intercedes for us? (Rom. 8:31-34).

So the self in its becoming-seeking-being is given ground and goal by the God-talk of the Christian faith. But the center of that faith speaks of what lies between ground and goal, the reality of human history. There Christian believers understand themselves to be not alone. Rather one lives "before" a God who has come. That this coming makes a difference to the self is indicated by Kierkegaard:

> [A] self directly before Christ is a self intensified by the inordinate concession from God, intensified by the inordinate ascent that falls upon it because God allowed himself to be born, become man, suffer and die, also for the sake of this self. . . . Qualitatively a self is what its criterion is. That Christ is the criterion is the expression, attested by God, for the staggering reality that a self has, for only in Christ is it true that God is man's goal and criterion or the criterion and goal.[30]

God as ground and goal for the gift of an ordering world. Similarly, Christian faith does not fail to connect with what we consider to be the "world." What is a "world" for? The person who travels to other places and the historian who studies other times both quest for a sustaining structure by which reality becomes accessible. With that structure, one can understand coherently and live creatively.[31] The "cosmological appeal" does not deal only with the echoing origin known to the astrophysicist pondering the "big bang" theory of the beginning of the world. It sounds fully as much in the still of the morning as quite ordinary individuals take up their lives anew.

There is more here than "quest." There is the haunting sense of giftedness. One senses that the world is a gift—that a world, life itself, is being given. In that gift there is order—not the order that crushes freedom, but the structure that supplies possibilities. The gift is ambiguous. We shall speak more of that presently, but it is clear that in the gift of life there is the gift of death. Nonetheless, the gift is gift, as even the second gift can serve the first. And the gift does not seem to be without point. Life is "for" something. Philosophers puzzle about the "anthropic principle" by which life seems directed and non-theists of several stripes offer ethical exhortations, whether in the public schools or in the halls of congress.[32] Thus the world leads us back to the self and its moral sense.

The Christian faith makes sense of this sense of giftedness and directedness. It speaks of the world as God's purposeful creation. There is gift in this: "The Lord is the everlasting God, the Creator of the ends of the earth. He does not faint or grow weary . . . He gives power to the faint." (Isa. 40:28-29) And there is the call to understand and to create. Anyone who makes sense of things does so *through* the world; people of faith make sense *of* it. That sense is most clearly realized in Jesus of Nazareth, in whom the will and promise of God are revealed in the flesh.

So there does seem to be a "fit" between the human self in the world and Christian God-talk. This is not the correspondence of a proof removing the need for faith, but faith can reach back to find an understanding, even if understanding in itself does not simply yield faith. Perhaps this gap can itself be understood, both from a general understanding of the human and from a specifically Christian perspective. Faith—any faith—seems to call the human person beyond reasoned analysis to willed commitment. That is the point of the philosophers who tell us that one cannot derive "ought" from "is." The Christian recognizes this and might call it an aspect of created freedom.

Power for the Future Through Incarnation and Resurrection

Thus the struggle to correspond finally points us to the third test of what can be true for human beings who in their finite freedom live and will their way into the future. Christian faith is challenged to offer power for the future in addressing finitude through incarnation and resurrection. Do Christian claims work? Does the gospel actually make free? Is there power to save here? The Christian gospel claims to be good news. If it does not save, it is not true. So the question must finally be: Does it save? All persons are entitled to press this question about themselves. We need to grant that some persons, probably through little fault of their own, have not found particular Christian claims to be saving. Christian spokespersons, whether clergy or lay, are challenged to speak precisely the fitting word to them. At midcentury Paul Tillich helpfully challenged the church to distinguish the differing anxieties among fate and death, emptiness and meaninglessness, and guilt and condemnation.[33] If "God" is a meaningless term for the hearer, it will not be helpful to pronounce the judgment of that God. Similarly, Dietrich Bonhoeffer warned in his later writings against the imposition of a particular "religious" solution upon a humankind "come of age."[34] We Christians still need these warnings.

But the question of the saving truth of Christianity is finally a much larger matter than the matter of fitting the Christian medicine to the individual's quite particular disease. In the Pannenberg passage cited in the previous section, it is asked whether the Christian faith still contains the truth that gathers everything together, everything experienced as real. That is the right question. We need to meet individual needs, but crucially the truth question is the question of the whole. What is the problem? There is a moral problem, of course. Against such evil we use moral persuasion and moral coercion. We impose the law and we offer love. But,finally, even in the moral realm there seems to be an element of necessity which must be addressed. We believe Paul's confessional words: "I do not do the good I want, but the evil I do not want is what I do" (Rom. 7:19). Hence the testimony of the tormented poet, John Berryman: "The only really comforting reflection is not we will all rest in Abraham's bosom and rot of that purport but: after my death there will be *no more sin.*"[35]

The problem seems ultimately to be metaphysical. It has to do with the way things are: with us in our sinning, yes; but even with reality itself in its very being. This may be an insight we could learn from the East. But it is something which can be clear to us in the Western categories with which we are all too familiar. How are self and world, self and others, finally to be reconciled? How are they to be one? We wage our rivalries, heralding now subjectivity, then objectivity.[36] This may not at first sound like a particularly religious problem, though in the threat of the finite other we may fear the judgment of the One who is Other than all of us. In any case the problem is not narrowly religious; it has to do not merely with the twistedness of our sinning but with the finite rootedness of our humanity.

Self and world are together in history. A gospel that would truly be saving for self and world will have to do with history. More than that, it must speak of the end of history. Another historical phase would not resolve a problem rooting in the very components of history. To what end will history come? Will there be an outcome? That which would save must deal with the temporality we feel in our bones, and yet it must do so in such a way that carries us to something which is not merely more of the same. Robert Jenson has written of this:

> Our acts threaten to fall between past and future, to become boring or fantastic or both, and all life threatens to become an unplotted sequence of merely causally joined events that happen to befall an actually impersonal entity, "me." Human life is possible only if past and future are somehow bracketed, only if their disconnection is somehow transcended, only if our lives somehow cohere to make a story. Life in time is possible only, that is, if there is "eternity," if no-more, still, and not-yet do not exhaust the structure of reality. Thus, in all we do we seek eternity.[37]

Another way to identify the poles of the problem is to speak of necessity and possibility. We live within and between these two and wonder at their outcome. The two are together in history, and we ask the end of history. A true answer cannot have to do with merely the one or the other. That which heals history, which fulfills history, which saves history must not be mere necessity. We know enough of necessity. We sense that our dying serves the living of others in the whole, if not in every particular, but the grim monotony of this circle does not save. That matter decays into energy is no cosmic gospel. Similarly, it will not avail to flee to bare possibility. The fantasy (impossibility?) of mere possibility—as in the astronomer's vision of intergalactic colonization or the religious vision of streets of gold—these will not save.[38] Something else is needed.

Necessity and possibility, self and world, are together in freedom. The metaphysical problem can be addressed only by that which is the fruit of freedom. Must we settle for saying with Sartre that the human being is a useless passion, or whistle through the graveyard of history with the hope that to recognize a boundary is to be beyond it? Perhaps not. Perhaps there is something more than the conjunction of opposites. That is the Christian proposal.

The Christian proposal is that the problem of all that which is not God has been met by God. The problem—and it matters not whether it be stated morally or metaphysically—has been met by God within the raw particularity of ordinary history. This God is truly other, and yet this God—so the story goes—has truly come. This claim speaks of God "tasting death for everyone" (Heb. 2:9).

One might try to fill out the proposal in terms like this:

> As surely as God is one we may be sure that within the reality that is God this suffering does not lurch about in uncontrolled abandon or throb on in inconclusive perpetuity. In freedom and love God chooses to be for us, to come to be with us, and so to suffer all that such identification entails. . . . here is will—not only to suffer, but in suffering. Thus there is here an actual advance in the life of God who undergoes—in an undergoing that is an undertaking—all that finitude and sin hold for us. As surely as God is one, no more than this is needed. It is enough; it is finished. God's will prevails. That is, God still wills to love, and the will that thus emerges from the event of Jesus is the eternal will that has worn the flesh of creation and crucifixion—once and so forever.[39]

Such an event could save self and world, could reconcile possibility and and necessity. This would make some actual difference to those who are caught up in the power of the event. Rowan Williams has put it this way: " 'God' is that to which all things are present, so theology traditionally affirms; so, through the mediation of God, all things can be made present to us again, present through his presence."[40] Hence the lives of Christians will bear some witness, as by their fruits they too are known (Matt. 7:16). I speak of actual difference to those "caught up" in the event, for the free act of God in Christ does not deal with the problem of necessity and possibility by obliterating one or the other. Both may still be discerned. There is still some contingency in the outcome, it would seem. And yet there is something at work here before and beyond our choosing. If some obdurate sinner does not want the love of God, that does not change God. There may be both triumph and tragedy in the love of God, suffering and joy, but history ends in the love of God.

IS THIS FRAMEWORK FAIR TO OTHER FAITHS?

But we are not at history's end. The visionary cadences of Christian faith carry us toward the end, but the reality of human finitude reminds us that we are very much in the middle of things. And here in this middle, Christian faith is clearly one faith among many in the Mainville of our lives. After all, were that not the case, there would be no need for this book. The Christian faith must be presented in these pages as one faith among many faiths increasingly coming into contact, and yes, competition. Therefore, it seems worthwhile for the Christian to try to state what is being said when truth is claimed for the Christian vision (version?) of things. But of course the Christian does not stop being Christian in doing this. May it be that the Christian is caught here in a vicious circle? Does the Christian actually specify what counts as truth in full dependence on the Christian faith and then, miracle of miracles, discover that it is the Christian faith which is true?

That may be the case. Clearly the Christian does not cease being a Christian when asked what it means for something to be true. Yet logicians distinguish between "vicious" and "virtuous" circles. In the virtuous circle the starting point is open to questioning and reformulation as the construction of the claim proceeds. How shall we know whether the Christian account of what it means to claim truth is virtuous or vicious? It does not seem sufficient for the Christian to consider this question without asking what other faiths make of the question of truth. Of course, it is still the Christian who asks, who listens. But it does not seem less circular to assume that in asking and listening the Christian cannot hear anything which is truly other. The venture seems worth the effort.

Other Faiths and Coherence

The challenge from the East makes clear that the test of coherence will carry weight only when set in relation to the actual finite life of faith before the Infinite. What, then, of these criteria—what of coherence, correspondence, saving power for the future? Are these recognized and accepted by the other faiths so that a significant dialogue can begin aiming at discerning true faith? Consider the matter of coherence. Is this criterion accepted beyond Christian faith? Perhaps in this book we may seem to be claiming that this test is not only accepted by the several faiths but even that it is passed by them. After all, we begin by identifying what we take to be "core intuitions" of the faiths. There is a "core," there is some kind of unity or cohesiveness here. Still, it could be an internally contradictory core. A given faith might consistently present a self-contradictory vision. Indeed, it might claim that just this character of self-contradiction is what is meant in this faith when "truth" is claimed. Hence to speak of faiths with core intuitions is not to conclude that they take and pass the test of coherence in one giant step.

In his study of Christianity, Islam, Hinduism, and Buddhism, Harold Coward notes that in each case reason and experience are claimed as verifying agents.[41] So far, so good for the criterion of coherence, one might suppose. But how far do we come if we find several faiths making favorable mention of "reason"? Are we speaking of a coherence characterizing the "propositions" of the faiths? We might be hopeful about that as we consider "religions of the book," Judaism, Islam, and Christianity. But we have a more complicated situation as we turn to the East. Hinduism is a notable case in point. Sarvepalli Radhakrishnan puts it so:

> While the East believes that there are realities which cannot be clearly seen, and even assumes that logical attempts to formulate them in communicable propositions do violence to them, the West demands clearness and is shy of mystery. What is expressed and is useful for our immediate ends is real, what is inexpressible and useless is unreal.[42]

Or, again, Sri Aurobindo wrote:

> But the Absolute, obviously, finds no difficulty in world-manifestation and no difficulty either in a simultaneous transcendence of world-manifestation; the difficulty exists only for our mental limitations which prevent us from grasping the supramental rationality of the co-existence of infinite and the finite or seizing the nodus of the unconditioned with the conditioned. For our intellectual rationality these are opposites; for the absolute reason they are interrelated and not essentially conflicting expressions of one and the same reality.[43]

Similarly, it may not be surprising to find Hindu writers minimizing the value of language. In his famous essay "The Mahatma and the Missionary," Gandhi says: "Your whole life is more eloquent than your lips. Language is always an obstacle to the full expression of thought."[44] Accordingly one will not be surprised by a Hindu suspicion over against creeds: "Creeds and dogmas, words and symbols have only instrumental value. . . . The name by which we call God and the rite by which we approach Him do not matter much."[45]

Something of the same challenge to the coherence criterion can be discerned in Buddhism. In her study of *The Buddhist Philosophy of Assimilation,* Alicia Matsunaga has this to say:

> Throughout the history of Mahayana Buddhism we find an inseparable relationship between *prajna* (wisdom) and *upaya* (skillful means).*Prajna,* in this instance, is synonymous with *sunyata, Pratitya samnutpada* (relativity) and *tathata* (that which is as it is). In other words, it denotes THAT which is obscured by discriminative reasoning. As we have earlier seen, these terms are

> not mere philosophical descriptions or speculations about the nature of the universe but rather concepts inseparably related to religious experience.[46]

Or, in a more popular statement once again, D. T. Suzuki, that well-known exponent of Zen Buddhism, could say this:

> What we are to realize, then, is the meaning of "Knowledge" and "Innocence," that is to say, to have a thoroughly penetrating insight into the relationship between the two opposing concepts—Innocence and Original Light on the one side, and Knowledge and Ignorance on the other. In one sense they seem to be irreducibly contradictory, but in another sense they are complementary. As far as our human way of thinking is concerned, we cannot have them both at the same time, but our actual life consists in the one supporting the other, or better, that they are inseparably co-operating.[47]

What are we to make of this? Perhaps we are best advised to avoid letting the test of coherence stand by itself in independence from other concerns. Somewhat similarly, we found Christian faith recognizing that coherence is at best an insufficient test for truth. Even Christians do not fail to speak of—or, perhaps more consistently, follow—the "way of negation," by which confidence in propositions gives way to another kind of knowing. Moreover, persons of several faiths seem to want to speak of the infinite and the finite together. It matters, of course, whether one supposes that to do that one must reject the criterion of coherence or whether one quests for a richer meaning for coherence, involving the believer's life in relationship to the transcendent. In such talk of experience we seem to move toward the correspondence criterion.

Other Faiths and Correspondence

The other faiths do make a claim about reality but understand that reality in differing ways, so that the "correspondence" is construed in different ways. Do the other faiths understand truth as a relationship in which human claims refer to a reality existing independently of the claiming? Is experience understood as the vital link between propositions and the reality to which they are supposed to correspond? "Experience" is one of the most elusive words in the dictionary of life, and we should not be surprised to find it used variously in the world's great religions.

Of course the faiths *involve* experience, as surely as they are actual ways of living in the world. But here we are inquiring about how they *regard* experience as they set about to speak of truth. In Gandhi's essay already cited, he speaks of "the spiritual world in the shape of direct experiences common to all faiths" and goes on to say:

> If we were to put the spiritual experiences together, we would find a result that would answer the cravings of human nature. Christianity is 1900 years old, Islam is 1300 years old; who knows the possibility of either? I have not read the Vedas in the original, but I have tried to assimilate their spirit and have not hesitated to say that, though the Vedas may be 13,000 years old—or even a million years old—as they well may be, for the word of God is as old as God Himself, even the Vedas must be interpreted in the light of our experience.[48]

What kind of experience is involved in the Christian understanding of truth as correspondence? In the previous section we spoke of how Christians understand our God-talk to connect with what we know apart from God. We spoke of God as ground and goal for self- and moral-directedness and for the gift of an ordering world. Is that of a piece with the "direct experience" Gandhi discovers in all faiths? Experience is not simply one—that much is clear. Paul Martinson contrasts Buddhist and Confucian accounts in these terms:

> Buddhist epistemology diverges considerably from the Confucian account. In particular, where the Confucian account . . . affirms a continuity of natural and moral (transcendent) knowing, the Buddhist account asserts a discontinuity between natural and transcendent knowledge, and therefore posits an epistemological dualism. This becomes the foundation stone for the Buddhist enlightenment or mystic quest.[49]

This should not surprise us. If the core intuition of Buddhism leads to the realization that "the idea of a permanent self is the product of ignorance," if the core intuition of Hinduism is escape to the real, we may not expect to find truth referring to the self-world relationship in these faiths. Other faiths may follow the Confucian tendency to link the natural and the transcendent. Thus Harold Coward notes Islam's claim to reasonableness, adding that "the idea that the Qur'an contains verifiable scientific data is often cited as something that places Islam above all other religions."[50]

Yet we must not make the contrast too clean. A prominent Japanese Buddhist scholar, Masae Abe, has argued that it is the Buddhist vision that is compatible with modern science, because it avoids the personalistic "dead-ends" of Western religious thought. He expounds the Buddhist notion of "dependent co-origination" in this passage:

> Christianity provides a positive answer to the question "why" in terms of the will of God. Even when human reason does not understand why something happens in a certain way, faith in God accepts it as a trial or the mercy of God. In contrast, Buddhism, in answer to the question "why," responds with "it is so without why" or "it is just as it is." "Without why" as an answer to the question "why" is quite compatible with the modern scientific mechanistic answer to the question "how."[51]

Similarly, in actual present existence Buddhist thought recognizes the place of self-talk. Thus Abe notes how nirvana takes place not in the race as a whole, but in individual human existence:

> The realization of transmigration is a personal realization for one's self, not for human existence in general. Apart from one's self-realization there can be no "problem" of birth-and-death, generation-and-extinction. Only through one's self-realization one can attain *nirvana* by solving the problem of generation-extinction, i.e., the problem of *samsara*.[52]

There does, then, seem to be talk of "correspondence" in the other faiths, though that talk is not single-minded in speaking of the reality to which claims are to be referred. Some distinction seems to exist between religions of "continuity" and religions of "discontinuity" at this point. Yet even this distinction cannot be made simply. In the previous section we suggested that perhaps the Christian struggle to correspond finally points us to the third test of what can be true for freedom. As we have tried here to speak of the reality to which the claims of other faiths are understood to refer, we seem to be driven once again to that third test. Do the other faiths recognize that religious truth is finally a matter of the power to save?

Other Faiths and the Power to Save

Other faiths join the Christian in looking to the power to save and in the quest to know that power. In the articles in this book we have claimed that all the great faiths look to salvation. We have said that we do not merely share the "primary continuities" of life, but also "the experience of a 'break' in these continuities." This does seem so and it seems significant. Masao Abe can draw together in this theme two religions as unlike as Christianity and Buddhism. ". . . Buddhism as a religion is essentially concerned with human salvation. In this respect there is no difference between Christianity and Buddhism, for both traditions are equally concerned with salvation."[53] Of course, Abe goes on to emphasize that the "foundation on which salvation becomes possible is differently understood." That too is significant, and we must not be misled by merely verbal resemblances. So we ask, are the religions together in saying that the question of truth cannot be settled by looking to the inner coherence of statements or the correspondence of those statements to the reality of the present? In claiming the truth do the religions make a statement about what is to come?

At least this seems clear: The life of the believer will not go unchanged. We noted above that even the less personalistic of the faiths do not fail to engage the individual on the way to liberation from the illusion of selfhood. Islam, of course, places a great emphasis upon the ethical engagement of the individual, so much so that Christian talk about grace becomes problematic. This concern is clearly present in Confucian thinking as well. But we have had occasion in these pages to think not only of Islamic surrender and Confucian *li* and *jen*, but also of Hindu dharma and of the "Eightfold Path" of Gautama Buddha. It is important, of course, not to trivialize the differences in these understandings. But it is important as well to recognize the significant degree to which the faiths seem to be together in saying "by their fruits you shall know them."

So far we have spoken of how the faith comes to bear on the self of the adherent. The faiths seem to be together in saying that the truth of the faith cannot be understood apart from this. But is there another "coming" of which truth speaks? Is there something out beyond the individual, something of the sort we found Christian faith proposing in what must be said to entail a metaphysically changed future?

Judaism and Islam in principle confront this issue inasmuch as they are teleological religions—they look for the decisive in the reality of history. They do so very differently from Christianity, of course. And in that difference they differ from each other, one might say. With Judaism, of course, the decisive is still awaited. Islam, on the other hand, sweeps past Jesus in its doctrine of abrogation (*naskh*) by which it is claimed that a prophetic revelation occurring later in time superseded an earlier one. Obviously, these are major differences. Yet the truth is in each case to be understood in and through the reality of historical coming.

This is, of course, less apparent in the Eastern faiths. There is a kind of "epistemological" coming which rivals the Western in its radicality. And yet even here there may be a haunting sense in which the faithful look to some kind of coming. Masao Abe has described such a challenge for Buddhist faith:

> The crucial task for Buddhism is this: How can Buddhism on the basis of "without why" as its ultimate ground formulate a *positive direction* through which ethics and history can develop? In other words, how can a *new teleology* be established on the ground of "suchness," which is neither teleological nor mechanical?[54]

This is not the place to consider Abe's proposal for that new teleology, though it may be noted that he appeals to the notion of compassion in seeking a foundation for such a Buddhist teleology. But it may be remarked that given the metaphysical cast of Hindu and Buddhist thought, such a proposal should not be a total surprise to Western readers. But where should such proposals, surprising or not, be considered? Precisely in the genuine interaction of mutual witness, one must say. And that is where the question of truth will be central. Perhaps one can even hope for some genuine community in this, the kind of community which seems to be sought in the religions of humankind. To this interaction the faiths bring varying degrees of missionary zeal. But even Hinduism, that most eclectic of faiths, recognizes that the truth is at stake—and at risk—in this. Carl Braaten has proposed that the reality of Jesus can be the basis of the conversation among the faiths. In his "Hindu View of Christ" Swami Akhilananda recognizes that when it comes to incarnation all things are not the same:

> We may say that it is evident that the Hindu view is closer to Christian orthodoxy than to "liberalism." The Hindu will agree with the orthodox in regarding Christ as unique in comparison with ordinary men; yet he will differ in holding that there have been and will be numerous incarnations of God. The Hindu would reject the view of those Christian liberals who regard all men as equally divine, Christ no more than anyone else.[55]

Between the engaged self and the final realization the faiths may together come to a conversation concerning the truth that matters most of all.

CONCLUSION

We must conclude that the Christian lives in the confident hope that this Christian faith indeed holds the truth that will make us free.

Much, much more could be said and needs to be said. Indeed Paul Martinson says much more in the next chapter. But what has been said seems to me to suggest that the Christian claim does fit the shape of the problem. It could be true. Is it true? Perhaps we do better to ask "*Will* it be true?" As humans we recognize that some truth claims can only be tested in the outcome. And if the Christian claim deals with the whole—that whole which cries out for salvation—then its truth will not be fully apparent in the middle of things. And yet this is no complete escape hatch to the future. The Christian claim is that the final future has already dawned; the decisive act has taken place, the kingdom is growing secretly. How secretly? Well, it can be known. This is the word of Jesus: "If you continue in my word, you are truly my disciples, and you will know the truth, and the truth will make you free" (John 8:31-32). So we seek to continue. As part of that we bear a witness to the word, even while we know that we do not yet possess fully that to which we bear witness. And we believe that this word will be true, that this truth will make us free.

Notes

1. Martin Luther, *The Bondage of the Will*, trans. J. I. Packer and O. R. Johnston (Westwood, N.J.: Fleming H. Revell Co., 1957), 67.
2. See the discussion by Roland E. Miller in *The Sending of God* (Calgary, Alberta: Concord Canada, 1980), esp. chapter 1.
3. *Luther's Works*, (Philadelphia: Muhlenberg, 1957), 31: 40.
4. Alfred North Whitehead, *Modes of Thought* (New York: The Free Press, 1938, 1966), 40-41.
5. Sigmund Freud, *The Future of an Illusion*, trans. James Strachey (New York: Norton, 1961), esp. 33.
6. John B. Cobb Jr., *Christ in a Pluralistic Age* (Philadelphia: Westminster, 1975), 19.
7. Thomas Kuhn, *The Structure of Scientific Revolutions* (Chicago: University of Chicago Press, 1982, 1970); Richard Rorty, *Philosophy and the Mirror of Nature* (Princeton: Princeton University Press, 1979); for Maturana, see the interview in *Networker*, May-June, 1985, 32-43. Cf. also Paul Watzlawick, ed., *The Invented Reality* (New York: Boston, 1984).
8. I take this phrase from John Hick's book, *God Has Many Names* (Philadelphia: Westminster, 1980, 1982). Hick seems to anticipate the movement from pluralism into relativism. His principle for reconciling faith differences is the Thomistic dictum: "The thing known is in the knower according to the mode of the knower."
9. Carl E. Braaten, "The Person of Jesus Christ," in *Christian Dogmatics*, ed. Carl E. Braaten and Robert W. Jenson (2 vols; Philadelphia: Fortress, 1984), 1: 567-68.
10. World Council of Churches, *Guidelines on Dialogue with People of Living Faiths and Ideologies* (Geneva: WCC, 1979), 3.
11. Dietrich Bonhoeffer, *Ethics*, ed. Eberhard Bethge, trans. Neville Horton Smith from the sixth German edition (New York: Macmillan, 1955; paperback ed., 1965), 195.
12. Wolfhart Pannenberg, *Basic Questions in Theology*, trans. George H. Kehm (Philadelphia: Fortress Press, 1971), 2: 1-2.
13. See John Austin, *How To Do Things With Words* (New York: Oxford University Press, 1965, 1973); and, for a theological appropriation, Donald Evans, *The Logic of Self-Involvement* (London: SCM, 1963).
14. William James, *Pragmatism: A New Name for Some Old Ways of Thinking* (New York: Longmans, Green, 1907), 201 (italics his).

15. Karl Barth, *Church Dogmatics*, trans. G. T. Thomson (Edinburgh: T. & T. Clark, 1936), I/1 (*The Doctrine of the Word of God*): 284-330.
16. Karl Rahner, *Theological Investigations*, trans. Cornelius Ernest (Baltimore: Helicon Press, 1961), 1: 149.
17. Paul Varo Martinson, *A Theology of World Religions* (Minneapolis: Augsburg, 1987), 200 (Hereafter cited as *World Religions*).
18. *Luther's Works*, (St. Louis: Concordia, 1968), 29: 216. Consider also this passage from Luther (*Weimar Ausgabe*, 23:157) that Bonhoeffer quotes in *Act and Being* (New York: Harper, 1956), 81: "It is the honor and glory of our God however, that, giving himself for our sake in deepest condescension, he passes into the flesh, the bread, our hearts, mouths, entrails, and suffers also for our sake that he be dishonourably handled, on the altar as on the cross."
19. Paul Tillich, *Theology of Culture*, ed. Robert C. Kimball (New York: Oxford University Press, 1959), 10 (italics his). Tillich's own preference is clear.
20. See Fritjof Capra, *The Turning Point* (New York: Simon and Schuster, 1982).
21. Cf. Michael Polanyi, *Personal Knowledge* (Chicago: University of Chicago Press, 1958) and Stephen Toulmin, *The Uses of Argument* (Cambridge: At the University Press, 1964). Or one could recall the distinctions Martin Buber made between "I-Thou" and I-it" relationships.
22. Simone de Beauvoir, *Ethics of Ambiguity*, trans. Bernard Frechtman (New York: Philosophical Library, 1948), 129.
23. Daniel Taylor, *The Myth of Certainty* (Waco, Tex.: Word Books, 1986), 106 (italics his).
24. *Luther's Works* (Philadelphia: Fortress, 1972), 33: 145-46.
25. Søren Kierkegaard, *Philosophical Fragments*, ed. H. V. Hong, trans. David Swenson (Princeton: Princeton University Press, 1962), 44.
26. For a development of this theme, see Terence Fretheim, *The Suffering of God: An Old Testament Perspective* (Philadelphia: Fortress, 1984).
27. See, for example, Herbert W. Richardson, *Toward an American Theology* (New York: Harper & Row, 1967), esp. chapter 5.
28. J. P. Sartre, *Being and Nothingness*, trans. Hazel Barnes (New York: Philosophical library, 1956), 615.
29. Peter L. Berger, *A Rumor of Angels* (Garden City, N.Y.: Doubleday Anchor, 1970), 66-68.
30. Søren Kierkegaard, *The Sickness Unto Death*, ed. and trans. Howard V. Hong and Edna H. Hong (Princeton: Princeton University Press, 1980), 113-14.
31. I have discussed this sense of "world" in *God: The Question and the Quest* (Philadelphia: Fortress Press, 1985), chapter 6.
32. On the "anthropic principle" see John Leslie, "Anthropic Principle, World Ensemble, Design," *American Philosophical Quarterly* 19:2 (April, 1982), 141-151 and *Nature* (Feb, 1984). A classic discussion on the "Is/Ought" matter is John R. Searle's in *Theories of Ethics*, ed. Philippa Foot (New York: Oxford University Press, 1967), 101-14.
33. Paul Tillich, *The Courage To Be* (New Haven: Yale University Press, 1965), chapter 2.

34. Dietrich Bonhoeffer, *Letters and Papers from Prison*, ed. Eberhard Bethge, trans. Reginald Fuller (New York: Macmillan, 1953, 1967).
35. John Berryman, "Surveillance," *The Ohio Review* 15 (Winter, 1974): 45 (italics his). This posthumuously published piece begins, "Almost the only place I really enjoy praying is hospital."
36. For a fuller discussion, see Sponheim, *God: The Question and the Quest*, chapter 7.
37. Robert W. Jenson, *The Triune Identity* (Philadelphia: Fortress Press, 1982), 1-2.
38. See Carl Sagan's *Cosmos* (New York: Random House, 1980) and Walker Percy's response in *Lost In the Cosmos: The Last Self-Help Book* (New York: Farrar, Straus, and Giroux, 1983), 172-4: "Sagan is lonely because, once everything in the Cosmos, including man is reduced to the sphere of immanence, matter in interaction, there is no one left to talk to except other transcending intelligences from other worlds."
39. Sponheim, *God: The Question and the Quest*, 132-3.
40. Rowan Williams, *Resurrection* (London: Darton, Longman & Todd, 1982), 23.
41. Harold Coward, *Pluralism: Challenge to World Religions* (Maryknoll, New York: 1985), 87.
42. Sir Sarvepalli Radhakrishnan, "East and West in Religion," in *Christianity: Some Non-Christian Appraisals*, ed. David W. McKain (New York: McGraw-Hill, 1964), 21 (Hereafter cited as *Christianity*).
43. "The Response of Sri Aurobindo and the Mother" by R. N. Minor, in *Modern Indian Responses to Religious Pluralism*, ed. by Harold G. Coward (Albany: State University of New York Press, 1987), 89.
44. Mohandas Karamchand Gandhi, "The Mahatma and the Missionary," in McKain, *Christianity*, 89.
45. Coward quotes this statement by Radhakrishnan in *Pluralism*, 77.
46. Alicia Matsunaga, *The Buddhist Philosophy of Assimilation* (Tokyo: Monumenta Nipponica, 1969), 113.
47. Daiseta Teitaro Suzuki, "Knowledge and Innocence," in McKain, *Christianity*, 123.
48. Gandhi, *op. cit.*, 81.
49. Martinson, *World Religions*, 46-47.
50. Coward, *Pluralism*, 54.
51. Masao Abe, *Zen and Western Thought*, ed. William R. LaFleur (Honolulu: University of Hawaii Press, 1985), 247-8.
52. Abe as cited in *Absolute Nothingness: Foundations for a Buddhist-Christian Dialogue* by Hand Waldenfels, trans. J. W. Heisig (New York: Paulist, 1976, 1980), 109.
53. Abe, *Zen and Western Thought*, 246.
54. *Ibid.*, 248.
55. Swami Akhilananda, "Hindu View of Christ," in McKain, *Christianity*, 56.

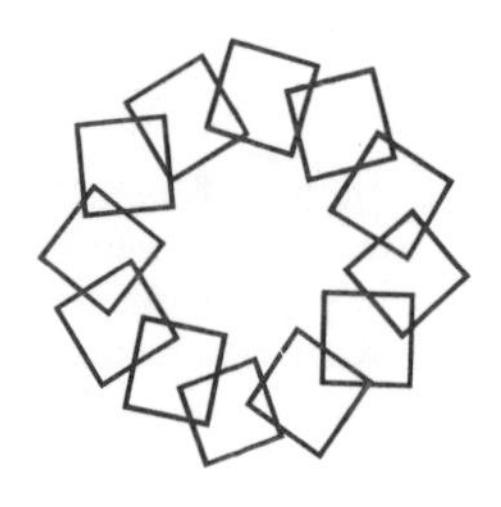

5

WHAT THEN SHALL WE DO?

Paul Varo Martinson

What then shall we do with all insights of the previous chapters in this book? Who is this "we" that are to do something? It is, of course, the church.

THE CHURCH THAT DOES

Congregations of the Evangelical Lutheran Church in America subscribe to the Augsburg Confession in their church constitutions. According to that Confession, the church is defined as "the assembly of saints in which the Gospel is taught purely and the sacraments are administered rightly."[1]

This definition is helpful, but only partially so. It is helpful because it makes clear that the church is a community of persons in which a very specific public action—proclamation of the gospel—takes place. The essential mark of the church is a public mark, there for all to see and hear. In our regular assembling together we are, warts and all, a public invitation for everyone about us to come and hear the Word.

But it is a partial definition because it does not make the inner dynamic of the church equally clear. The inner dynamic is a hidden, unseen mark. Thus, the Reformers had to clarify the Augsburg Confession's definition. They made up for this lack in the Apology, to which our congregations also subscribe. In the Apology we read that "the church in the proper sense is the assembly of saints who truly believe the Gospel of Christ and who have the Holy Spirit."[2] Here the church is no longer defined strictly in terms of public practice. The church is both visible and not visible. Nobody can see faith or take the pulse of the Holy Spirit and thereby claim to detect the contours of "the assembly of saints."

There is, therefore, no way to talk intelligibly about the church, about who this "we" may be, without recognizing that it is a community that has both outwardly discernible public marks and inwardly dynamic, hidden marks. The church in a fuller sense thus comes into its own by a double movement. By the exercise of its public office of proclamation of the gospel, it gives rise to the hiddenness of faith; from the hiddenness of faith, it gives rise to the exercise of the public office. Of course, the church as public and the church as hidden are not quite the same thing. However, one cannot be had without the other.

There is another reason why the definition of the church in Article 7 of the Augsburg Confession is only partially helpful. It defines the church in terms of its "place," as the assembly "in which" something happens. While this too is necessary, it is not enough. The church can never be simply the gathered community "in" which something happens. It is as much, if not more, the place "from" which something happens. That means we need to understand the church as community of word and Spirit in terms of movement as well as in terms of position. Indeed, if we turn to the New Testament we soon find out that the church is by definition the community that comes into being by being sent. Jesus said, "As the Father has sent me, even so I send you"[3] (John 20:21).

The church exercises its public office by ceaselessly making the gospel available not only in the assembly of saints, but also in those assemblies where it has not yet been heard—whether that failure to hear is an audible failure (too far away to hear) or an existential failure (your deeds speak so loudly I can't hear your words). Thus, the public character of the church also has two aspects: it is an assembly that lives publicly before God and that, therefore, lives publicly for others. The praxis is always simultaneously twofold: worship and witness. Assembled the church continually hears and lives that Word, unassembled it speaks and lives the Word without ceasing. It is a community that bears the marks of the gospel; it is a sign of God's future for all.

The "we" are a community of faith in which there is a perpetual interdependence among the parts of its definition of itself. The church is (1) a public communal event of gospel proclamation, (2) which still remains hidden in faith, (3) as it lives dynamically for others. Only if we understand who we are in this kind of way can we even begin to address the question of "What then shall we do?"

What then shall we, this community, do? First of all, it might help to think clearly about the situation.

Three Phases of Relationship

If what we have said about the church is correct, then it cannot understand itself in the abstract. While we are not "of" the world (for the world is not the source of our life and faith) we are nonetheless "in" the world, part and parcel of it in such a deep way that we cannot sunder ourselves from the world any more than did the Lord. This means that we too are part and parcel of the world religions. We represent one among many. This study is geared to help us think through and experience afresh what this really means for us and our community of faith.

In the first chapter we began to think about this complex world of many religions. We have been introduced to the core intuitions of several religious communities. These intuitions bring to us insights and questions that are challenging, maybe interesting or appealing, perhaps even disturbing. Yet we need to acknowledge these invitations as commitments of real people in real communities in a real world.

Our relationship with those from other religious communities occurs in at least three phases: discovery of what we have in common; alertness to what is different; openness to change by enrichment or conversion. These phases are not chronological, as if one follows the other in a proper order. They are simultaneous, intermixing in many ways. The order in which I place them here is a theological order. It follows the order of the three articles of the Apostles' Creed that we confess Sunday after Sunday.

Discovery of the Common

We always welcome the discovery of the common in our ordinary relations—common friends, common relatives, common employment, common enjoyments. So too should it be in our relations with people of other faiths.

The biblical teaching on creation and revelation is the background for all Christian relations with peoples of other faiths. We share a common world, a common humanity, and certain common psychological, social, and economic dynamics. We also have life from a common transcendent source, so Christians believe, that we call God. All of creation is in relationship to this one God, and God is always dynamically present with the world, so that all of creation is in fact a revelation. That which is common, then, is deeper than our common humanity. It includes God's revealing activity. All people, religious or not, respond to this divine communication. Appropriate response to God is possible outside the church, wherever revelation occurs.

There are at least two crucial areas where we share things in common with other religious communities. One is in the experience of the primary continuities of life; another is in the experience of a break in these continuities.

Primary continuities are certain elements of human life so basic that we never get away from them. Nothing is more basic, for instance, than our relationship with the earth, or water,or the elements of the sky. Within these immediate realities we live and move and have our being. Even modern industrial society cannot get away from this basic continuity.

Another basic element is that of home, family, and employment. Without children the human race would become extinct. Without some kind of social organization it would be impossible for us to survive and function as individuals. Without a means of livelihood we would be impoverished outcasts or dependent on others' largesse.

Our relationship with nature and with our social environment is always precarious. The vagaries of nature in earthquake, storm, and drought are well known. The social calamities of strife and warfare are also well known. We have, like all humanity, a custodial concern for our well-being so that nature and society nourish and sustain us. This is a concern for the primary continuities of life. At the same time, it is universally recognized that we all do die, that society is depleted even as it procreates, and that we come from and return to nature.

Some religious traditions and ritual communities have core intuitions basically concerned with these primary continuities of our being. These religions are concerned with the sustaining powers of nature (e.g., fertility rites), or the supporting powers of society (e.g., ancestral veneration), or the inevitable rhythms of life and death (e.g., rites of passage from one state to another, both within life and beyond). The Christian community shares the custodial concerns expressed through rites such as these. We also express them in prayer, song, and liturgy.

Without a doubt, most of human religious life from time immemorial has been concerned with the quest for preserving these continuities. The custody of these continuities reflects the core intuition in each religion. Why not? After all, life here and now is the only life we have been given. How can anything be more important than what matters right now? Life is not to be escaped but to be lived as well and as fully as is possible. The ecological rhythms in our relations with nature are at risk; health, economic well-being, and progeny are also always at risk. Death and evil seem even to threaten not only our own well-being but even that of the cosmos itself. Shall the cosmos be destroyed with all that is in it? Because of these risks to the valued continuities of life, custodial rites arise.

In other religious communities the primary continuities of life—birth and death, nature and community—and the traditional ritual custodianship of them have undergone a severe shaking. The result is that discontinuities stand more boldly to the fore. As a consequence, core intuitions of these communities are being radically reshaped by the discontinuities.[3] For example, the experience of a sharp break in the continuities has taken place in the Middle East, in Israel, and in the Indian culture within Buddhism.

In India, for instance, the experience of human finitude and the suffering of human life became overwhelming concerns as seen in the emphasis upon *samsara* (the endless rounds of transmigration), the implacable law of karma which brought deserved suffering in its wake, and the quest for *moksha,* a final deliverance. Buddhism saw suffering in all its forms (physical, mental, cosmic) as the symptom of a profound break within the human consciousness itself. All these disturbances, the Buddha argued, arose from a basic human greed, rooted in self-centeredness.

This experience of a profound discontinuity within existence is something deep within the biblical and Christian experience as well. In this we share profoundly similar concerns with Buddhists and others.

Alert to the Difference

We must always be alert to difference. The common makes relationship possible; difference makes it significant. Generally people do not give their lives for that upon which we all agree or find we have in common. People give their lives because of that which is different. Difference is fraught with significance.

Every religion is unique. Who would argue that? But to go beyond this trivial observation and to clarify that which is unique and consider its significance is no longer trivial.

What is unique to the Christian faith? Or to put it another way, what does the Christian community have to offer to followers of all other religions? The answer is obvious—the story of Jesus. The Christian community alone grounds its life here. It is that story which is unique to us.

But Christians do not just repeat a story and leave it at that. It is repeated, to be sure; and life is lived on the basis of it, for a reason—for many reasons. It is a story with meaning and significance for life. It is here, in the saying and doing of this story, that the Christian witness takes on flesh and blood.

Buddhism, we discovered, has discerned a profound disturbance within human life—a life based on a greedy attachment to the world that arises from self-centeredness. The experience of this "break" in the continuities of life leads to a quest for liberation, to the discovery of a new and deepened continuity. This liberation the Buddha offers is a changed consciousness—a consciousness without the awareness of a self.

The Christian too discerns a break and discovers a liberation. But because the Christian sees this differently, and so sees liberation differently.

The Buddhist discovers a single break which is within human consciousness. However, the Christian, grounded in the biblical experience, discerns a double break. From the start the Bible pronounces a relationship between God and world, but a relationship in which there is a primal discontinuity: "In the beginning God created the heavens and the earth" (Gen. 1:1). God is not creature, and creature is not God. Life did not have its real source in the eternal rhythms of nature and cosmos; its source is God. Such a God cannot be compelled by the world nor appropriated by ritual and piety. This first "break," God's good creative act, is accompanied by a second. The story of the Fall showed a second "break," a deep discontinuity in the very heart and soul of humanity, not unlike the Buddhist insight into greed and self-centeredness, but grounded on the already given affirmation of creation.

This double break in the biblical experience (creation, Fall) does not permit a Buddhist solution, which lacks any teaching on creation. For the Buddhist the break was only a break in consciousness. It was a problem of perspective and attitude alone. By losing one's ego, by the changing of one's perspective, one could transcend the break and experience some kind of identification, mystical or otherwise, with the totality of things. But for the Christian, both breaks are real. Creation is real. God is not the world, and the world is not God; but God and the world are in relationship. Sin is also real. Sin is a human activity that has real consequences for both human and divine-human relationships. Liberation is achieved not by denying the reality of the break, not by a simple change of perspective, but by accepting God's descent of love in incarnation, death, and resurrection. This descent made the break internal to God's own reality—"in Christ" (i.e., in cross and resurrection) "God was reconciling the world to himself" (2 Cor. 5:19). By descent God became creature (John 1:1, 14); by descent God's Son became sin (2 Cor. 5:21). By descent God alone overcame the break. Change of perspective, our faith, is grounded in this.

Openness to Change

Being alert to that which is different, we are open then to change. We are witnesses—something we shall discuss shortly. Similarly, we will recognize that people of other religious commitments are also witnesses to us.

This exchange of witnessing is important. Other religious communities have important claims to put forward, and it is precisely from what is different in them that we have the potential of learning the most. This learning can only happen if we listen to their witness.

A witness purports to speak the truth, to witness to something other or greater than one's self. With such a motive, one seeks to present a winsome and convincing witness. If we are open to each other's witness, this clearly means the possibility of being persuaded by the witness of another. Where the witness of another is persuasive, we ought to heed. In heeding we will be changed.

But ought we to listen? Do we not already have the truth? Perhaps that is not well put. God's truth is greater than that we can encompass. We may not possess the truth. However, we do believe the truth has possessed us, and that in Christ. We have already seen that God is present to all, beyond the confines of synagogue or church, beyond the witness even of Torah and gospel. That which is common to us and all people is deeper than merely our common humanity. God's revealing will is disclosed to all. The gospel focuses that witness in a final, decisive, and climactic way. But it has not done so to destroy once and for all every other witness. When others speak we ought to listen, and in listening to change.

All kinds of change are possible. Maybe a false idea about the other, a careless cliché, will be blown away. Perhaps we will discover a new attitude, a new pattern of relating to others. Maybe new insights never before considered will come. We will learn. To learn is to change. Change may even mean conversion. Whether mutual witness brings about many "small" conversions (one remains in one's faith but holds it in a new or changed way) or a single "big" conversion (one ceases to be Christian and becomes Buddhist, or vice versa), change is sure to come. We need the articulation of the Christian faith anew in intimate interaction with the Hindu, Buddhist, Muslim, Jew, and other great religious commitments. We need their witness.

The Muslim shares with the Christian the sense of a double break—creation and Fall. Muslims, of course, do not find liberation in Jesus, for reasons stated earlier in this study. Why do we need to hear their witness, to learn and change?

If there is any besetting theological sin among Christians, it is to so speak and think of the divine descent that we end up making God in our image. We forget that in fact it is the other way around. We seek a God who meets all our felt needs. By making God servant to our needs, we forget the primal "break" between God and world given in creation. God's descent never annulled that break. What the descent did was to give creation heightened value while bringing pain to God. On the other hand, Islam, tirelessly asserting God's creative and revealing power, is a witness to the greater glory of God—*allahu akbar* (God is greater). Divine majesty is affirmed in the face of human frailty. Our worship and our witness can be "converted" anew to this greater glory as we heed this Muslim witness.

What paying heed to the witness of others—Muslim, Buddhist, Jew, Hindu, secular humanist, or atheist—could mean for our own formulation of the Christian faith can hardly be predicted ahead of time. Mutual witnessing is a process in which all the resources of past and present need to be brought to bear so that we continue to learn and to change. Such learning and changing can be a painful, disturbing experience. It is like our daily "washing" in the waters of baptism, a daily dying and rising. Yet through that disturbance comes greatest joy, for we are "changed into his [the Son's] likeness" (2 Cor. 3:18).

These three phases—finding that which is common, alertness to that which is different, openness to change—are a perpetual part of our response as we encounter people and communities whose core intuitions are not our own. To neglect any one of these phases is to court disaster. It is a failure to "discern the spirits." We are obligated to the whole counsel of God, including both God's creating and revealing as well as God's redeeming work as we anticipate the consummation.

Part of this counsel, as we have seen, is that which is unique to the Christian. The Christian community does have a witness, indeed, must witness. How do we speak of that?

PRACTICING THE RELATIONSHIP THROUGH WITNESS

Witness is the comprehensive term for our active relationship with people of other religious commitment. Witness is our mission, our sending, our commission. The mission is God's; the witness is ours. These terms include everything that a Christian community might do as a "Christian" community.

Witness, as we said earlier, means to bear testimony concerning something other than one's own self. Nevertheless, it implies direct experience. Testimony, because it relies upon direct experience and not public evidence, requires integrity. Thus it is that in the New Testament, a witness is a martyr—the word is the same. No greater integrity can be asked than the giving of one's life for the sake of one's testimony. Testimony, if the matter testified to is of any consequence, will include persuasion. Witnesses will seek to have their testimonies be warmly regarded and valued.

If the term witness is comprehensive, it will also be complex. We will therefore want to differentiate the term witness into its several layers of application. All that the Christian community as a mission community does in the public sphere is included in witness: worship,[4] evangelism, dialogue, participation.

Worship

Christian worship is a public event. There are no hidden secrets in religion here: It is not a secret rite. In worship the Christian community identifies its source. This source is God—the God of vulnerable love whose majesty is made manifest in cross and resurrection. We are baptized into the embrace of this God; we commune at the anticipatory feast prepared for us by the redeeming act of this God; we sing and pray and preach inspired by this God. This God we name Father, Jesus Christ, Holy Spirit.

The dynamic of this worship has two parts. One is *ad-intra*, an interior, private, dimension. It soaks into the depths of our communal life and would bring all into conformity with the cruciform mode of God's being with us. It reaches at the same time into the depths of our personal life, to bring about a personal conformation. Worship is first of all God's work, not ours. God calls us to worship and we come. God calls to us in the midst of worship and we repent and believe. Thus the church becomes a community of people transformed from within. This community is grounded in grace, the grace that forgiven people know.

But worship also has an *ad-extra* part. It is turned toward the outside. This "turning toward" occurs in at least three senses. Worship that is public seeks to become more inclusively public. The source of our worship is God, whose will is to embrace all, "who desires all . . . to be saved" (1 Tim. 2:4). God would embrace all in the waters of baptism; God would welcome all to the feast of the future; God would inspire all with the word of God's love. Worship that is public, moreover, seeks that the interior conformation to the cruciform mode be also the way of the church's presence in the world of everyday life. God's intensive love for the needy, the oppressed, even the evil, would become the church's intensive love for the weak and the oppressed.[5] Worship that is public, finally, seeks the inclusion of all that is good, praiseworthy, and edifying in its cultural setting as it promotes songs, prayers, and sermons appropriate to a given place and time. It is also open to all that is good in other religions, in other cultural traditions. The crossing of cultures, whether generational or communal, happens as the church worships. Each new generation has a different sense of music. Liturgy that lives is continually modified as it is enriched with the music of the people. In some cultures dance and drum are major forms of musical expression. Liturgy that lives will use these new forms in its continuing renewal. Worship that is public refuses to be the worship of a ghetto. It refuses to be simply foreign, or frozen in time, but insists on being lodged in the everyday experience of people.

The church is a community. Nurtured by the gospel, by Word and sacrament, knowing God's grace and favor, it becomes a community of love—mutual love and outgoing love. It is a sign, by God's grace, of God's coming kingdom of love.

Beyond this arises the question of common worship among members of different religions. Is there a place for this? What might this mean? Are there limits? Are there new possibilities? Are there appropriate ways in which we can share in some measure in the worship of others, and others with us?[6]

Evangelism

In the public offer of the gospel, which is evangelism, the church articulates in a public way that God is for others. The bottom line is that the church has nothing to offer the world except this gospel. It is the story this gospel tells that is unique to the Christian community.

For many the term "evangelism" has become problematic. There have been repeated calls for greater definitional clarity. It seems to be our current fashion to inflate the definition of almost every term we use so that it becomes a general, nonspecific category which allows us to say everything we have to say. The word "evangelism" has not escaped that inflation. One Lutheran, James Scherer, writes: "An updated terminology is needed to show the relationship between church renewal activities, 're-evangelization' of nominal Christians, evangelism as the activity of the local church, cross-cultural missions to unevangelized peoples, and church mission in its holistic and inclusive sense."[7] It is for the sake of the truly universal mission on which God sends us that we need particular clarity.

Evangelism is the public offering of the gospel, the evangel. But what is the heart of this evangel? It is the evangel of the divine commitment to relationship with the world. God created the world as a reality other than God's self that there might be relationship. "And God saw . . . that . . . it was very good" (Gen. 1:31). Yet, "sin came into the world through one man and death through sin, and so death spread to all men because all men sinned" (Rom. 5:12). Despite this rupture, through covenant and prophets this God remained committed to a relationship with this world in mutuality and freedom. This commitment reached the deepest participation possible with the world in the divine vulnerability we name Jesus Christ. The mode of God's commitment is cruciform: "For God so loved the world that he gave his only Son" (John 3:16); "God was in Christ reconciling the world to himself" (2 Cor. 5:19); "Since therefore the children share in flesh and blood, he himself likewise partook of the same nature" (Heb. 2:14). This commitment, moreover, shall find its consummation when all things shall be brought into subjection to God, that is, to God's love, "that God may be everything to every one" (1 Cor. 15:28). This is evangel; this is the evangelizing God; this is a commitment to relationship. Through evangelism the church expresses this commitment. The evangel is verbal.

But are we really moved to making of this public offer? In a reflective moment, James Scherer posed the issue this way: "Lutherans seem to lack one essential requirement for fulfilling their missionary task—a compulsive reason for sharing the good news of God's kingdom in Jesus Christ with others."[8] If this were indeed the case, one might almost think this reason enough to cease to be Lutheran. The "compulsive reason" lies in the gospel itself. If we Lutherans are moved by the gospel, then there is much to be done.

It is my conviction that everything in mission rises or falls with the congregation, the local community of faith, those who in some specific place live by Word and sacrament. This congregation is the whole church in microcosm. Because this is so, the congregation in its place is the responsible community that witnesses. It is here that primary evangelism takes place, that the concrete public offer of the gospel happens. If the congregation fails, the whole church fails. Only the congregation can reach the increasingly secularized West. Only the congregation can reach the vast growing communities of new immigrants, legal or illegal. Only the congregation that will pay the price of witness will have an effective outreach.

It is this act of witness, above all, that propels the church into relationship with the world. All agendas for the church are first discovered here in the congregation. Whatever is done in the church at large to bring about more effective witness must make the congregation a more effective subject of witness.

As one moves up in the organizational hierarchy, it seems that at each higher level a new subject of mission and witness appears which may often preempt the congregation's identity as the proper subject of witness. Nevertheless, no congregation can go it alone. To attempt to do so is theologically unsound. It is a fundamental denial of the congregation's own identity as a microcosm of the body of Christ.

Further, going it alone is equally unsound practically. As the congregation makes the public offer of the gospel, the world, including people of other faiths, will respond. Inevitably the world will interrogate the bringers of this gospel. It soon will become apparent that the issues raised cut across the entire spectrum of Christian existence. While response is inescapable, only a larger, gathered Christian response can be adequate. Rightly done, evangelism will always lead to dialogue, as well as to other modes of witness, in the struggle with these increasingly large and complex issues.

Dialogue

Dialogue is an expansion of the commitment to that relationship undergirding evangelism. There is often dispute about the compatibility of evangelism and dialogue—as if commitment to relationship can have only one form. Some find dialogue antagonistic to evangelism; some substitute dialogue for evangelism. In actual fact, commitment is variegated, multiform, rich.

To be sure, dialogue differs from evangelism. Evangelism is a public offering; dialogue is a public reasoning. The missionary Paul frequently moved between the dialogical and evangelical modes of witness. Dialogue arises from interrogation. With this in mind we might speak of four aspects of dialogue: its origins, its goal, its result, its practice.

Dialogue is always a secondary form of witness, because dialogue arises by reason of interrogation. The primary witness is assumed. But questions arise. Is this witness true? On what basis do you make such claims? Is it worthwhile? Does it relate to this or that? The questions come, and people of other faiths interrogate us, as we also interrogate them. Dialogue is one necessary result when a witness is called to account. This is its origin.

The goal of dialogue is simple. On the one hand it is to make a persuasive witness and, on the other, to heed a persuasive witness. Dialogue is not merely an exchange of information, neither is it merely a quest for understanding (though it surely involves both of these). Dialogue is a sharing of convictions. And to be persuasive, as Paul Sponheim suggested in the previous chapter, that witness must be coherent, relate to the actual world, and offer power for the future. Dialogue whose goal is any less than this—to make and to heed a persuasive witness—is less than full dialogue.

This, of course, has consequences for the result. What is the expected result of dialogue? It should be clear: The intended result of dialogue should be that the external dialogue is followed by internal dialogues of all parties concerned. Not until the interrogation and the shared convictions have been appropriated through an internal dialogue can dialogue be said to have had a good result. This internal dialogue may lead to many things. We have already spoken of change and learning, of "big" and "small" conversions. At least the latter will take place if the dialogue is internalized.

All this suggests a number of implications for the practice of dialogue. This includes at least the following: Dialogue is a venture; it requires integrity; it involves full mutuality.

All witness, indeed, is a venture. It is also the case with dialogue, for here one's witness is exposed in a public way to the sustained interrogation of those who find it incredible or puzzling, or perhaps interesting and attractive, or just simply wrong. To thus be exposed to interrogation truly calls witness to account. To enter dialogue requires the willingness to venture. It is, of course, of the nature of faith precisely to venture.

Dialogue requires integrity. Integrity assumes that one is well informed about one's faith and is a convinced participant in that faith. Further, genuine integrity requires one to be open to the witness that another might bring and to be willing to be persuaded by all that is convincing. Specific criteria as to what ought to be persuasive for all concerned in a dialogue cannot be set out beforehand. Their convictions help shape the criteria that count for each of them. Yet, the witness cannot be incoherent, irrelevant, and offer no help for the future. At the same time, integrity involves responsibility to a tradition for, after all, the real dialogue is between communities of faith. It is not enough to speak only from personal, perhaps idiosyncratic, convictions.

Dialogue involves full mutuality. This has been assumed throughout this whole discussion. To make and heed a persuasive witness requires mutuality. To let each participant be the final arbiter of that which characterizes one's own faith requires mutuality. To let dialogue move from the external to the internal phase requires mutuality. To venture is to expose oneself to the interrogation of the other. All of this depends on accepted mutuality.

While dialogue is one form of witness, it is not the only form. We have not spoken of disputation or debate. There has already been a long history of contentiousness among religious communities. Dialogue seeks to get behind all contention so as to be responsive to the intention of the core intuition that informs each faith community. At the same time, dialogue presupposes the primary witness that evangelism brings. The life of dialogue depends upon evangelism; evangelism without dialogue becomes divisiveness.

Dialogue must take place at several levels concurrently. The most important levels are the confessional, the ecumenical, and the inter-faith. So far, it seems, dialogue has been dominated by the ecumenical model, even when it takes place at different levels.

Lutherans have a particular obligation to take dialogue seriously. We need to be moved by external dialogue to a genuine internal dialogue. This can only happen, in the final analysis, at the confessional level. We need the interrogation of others. We know that the Lutheran Confessions were formulated in a day when it was assumed that all Europe was Christian. This assumption, of course, removed from the Christian community Jews and those Muslims who chanced to live in lands under European rule. None of these so-called non-Christians were taken seriously in their religious commitments. In terms of the understanding of mission today, our confessional documents often appear static. How do these time-honored formulations look now in the light of the interrogation that a Buddhist, a Muslim, a Hindu, or a Confucian might bring to them? A serious interrogation of our confessional tradition in the light of the interfaith dialogue is long overdue. Such an interrogation promises to deepen our insight into the very Confessions themselves. If we let this interrogation happen, it can become an important and potentially creative piece of the large ecumenical involvement in interfaith dialogue. For instance, what will happen to our formulation of the understanding of God as triune if we take the Muslim interrogation seriously? What will happen to our formulation of the doctrines on grace and faith if we take the Buddhist interrogation seriously? What will happen to our theology of creation if we take the Native American interrogation seriously?

Because dialogue has suffered at the confessional level, it has suffered drastically at the local level. How many Lutheran congregations around the world are engaged in creative, intentional dialogue with people of other faiths? The real desire seems often to be to keep them at a distance rather than to engage them in dialogue. Are we afraid of being interrogated? Do we not have our own theological house in sufficient order to venture?

Our fourth consideration on the modes of witness has to do with participation. We turn to that next.

Participation in the World

Not "of" the world, we are yet "in" the world, participators in the world's destiny. God's love is extensive, reaching to all equally and without favor. God's love is also intensive, reaching down as Jesus said "to the least of these"—the outcast, disfavored, oppressed, poor—with a particular intensity. Our participation is grounded on this double outreach to people, all kinds of people.

Primary witness as a public offer of the gospel is evangelism, a witness in word. This needs to be accompanied by the equally primary witness of work and life.

Now it is a basic characteristic of witness, we have seen, that it is not done for the self even if by the self. Its content is always alien; it is not what I am or do. Its purpose is always for the other. This is as true of witness in work as it is in word. Obviously, the whole range of issues—justice, poverty, peace, health, ecology—are integral to this witness in work.

Five circles of participation. A helpful way to envision our participation in the human agenda of this world is to think of our participation in five concentric circles. To get started, we might borrow some insights from the Confucian tradition. The Confucian speaks of five basic relationships that underlie all forms of human relationship. These include three familial relationships of parent and child, husband and wife, brother and sister; the wider social or civil relationships of friend and friend; and finally the political relationship of ruler and ruled.

In the first and most intimate circle in our diagram we would place the three familial relationships. This circle we might term kinship society, a circle of relationship in which values of intimacy and nurture are uppermost. The second wider social circle we might term civil society, the circle of relationships into which we enter daily in our ordinary pursuits. Above all the second circle includes the relationships of our economic life: our neighbors, our business relations, our occupational and professional relations, even our recreational relations. The dominant values sought in this circle of relationships are benefit values: health, wealth, and worth. The second circle is often experienced as a realm of competition.

Then there is the third circle of political society, ideally the realm in and through which we seek after the common good. The goal of the political world is to integrate into a functioning whole the many small and often competing worlds of kinship and civil society. The principle values here are justice values.

To push the diagram further, these three circles are within a fourth, even prior, circle of our involvement with nature. This we might term the ecological circle. Nature and society are continually interactive in countless ways. There are tensions between the two that are not easily resolved. Our world of society, which is at the same time our cultural life, necessarily involves us in the management of nature and its forces. Nature, in turn, is indifferent to our social and cultural pursuits and places constraints upon them, even while making them possible in the first place. The principal value of the ecological circle here we might term custodial.

Finally, there is a fifth circle, the cultural circle, that sums up all the others. Human cultures are the "webs of significance"[9] that we spin as we give meaning and value to our experience in all of the other circles and their interactions. Thus, the principal value of the cultural circle is meaning. Closely attached to this meaning are the forms through which cultural meaning is conveyed. However, various human cultural webs are spun on the basis of different and unique assumptions. Therefore, communication between them and understanding of each other among them is a profound challenge. If it is true that "religion is the meaning-giving substance of culture, . . . and culture is the form of religion,"[10] then we are aware of both the necessity and the difficulty of our involvement in cross-cultural discourses.

As a Christian community we live within all five circles at once. The values of intimacy and nurture are to be treasured; the benefit of neighbor and of self is to be sought; justice and freedom from oppression are to be achieved. At the same time, our superintendency of nature is essentially the role of custodian of gifts accorded to us. And all of this is wrapped up in the forms and meanings that we give to life and that shape our own realities from inside out.

To live at the point of juncture where all these circles center is far from easy. Indeed, it will be a struggle. The contemporary issues involving race, sex, poverty, life-style, and the unborn, to mention only some of the most obvious, are part of this struggle. Yet, it is only in the midst of the struggle that we will experience grace.

We dare not be identified fully with any one of these circles, but we dare not fail to participate in all of them to the utmost of our abilities. Were we to be identified overmuch with kinship society, we would risk becoming a tribal or ethnic religion. Both the Holocaust and Middle Eastern wars instruct us well in this regard. Were we to be identified overmuch with civil society, we would risk becoming another corporation. The recent fate of some TV evangelists and the increasing corporate structure of the church instruct us well in this regard. Were we to be identified overmuch with political society, we would risk ceasaropapism or revolutionary romanticism. Iran's Khomeini has taught us afresh the danger of the first; both he and Mao Tse-tung have taught us the meaning of the latter. Were we to be identified with nature overmuch, we would lose social coherence and revert to a primitive anarchism. Utopian socialist experiments have taught us much in this regard. But neither can we opt out of participation in any of these circles to become an alternative community standing over against a world of evil. We then risk becoming just another sect. Our history is full of instruction in this problem too.

In the world but not of the world, the church is thus sent into the world (John 17:11, 16, 18). The world is not culturally tamed, yet it is culturally relevant. The church must ever be a meaning-giving agent within culture, each culture. Commitment to relationship identifies that which lies at the root of both our word and work in the world, for it is God's commitment to be related to us that has established us in grace. Therefore God also has reconciled us and freed us to build relationships. We are bonded to these circles by loving will for all humanity.

Interrogation. We have spoken earlier of the interrogation brought to us by people of other faiths. Precisely at this point of participation in the various circles some of the most disturbing and insistent questioning is pursued. It is a fact of history that the Christian community has not always, perhaps seldom, lived well amidst these several circles. We have not participated as we should. Our words may be well chosen, but our work has often been badly done.

We need not go far to encounter this interrogation. Our own nation is founded in a not insignificant part upon the systematic, often brutal, destruction of Native American peoples and their cultures. Their blood still cries from the ground today. A recently awakened native American community becomes the coherent voice for this hitherto muffled and incoherent cry which stings our ears. The blacks and our slave-owning past, the Asians and our prejudiced past, the Hispanics and our indifferent past, all cry out together against us.

Our Muslim neighbors have not and will not forget the religious crusades of the past. For many of them, it is as though it took place yesterday. The modern colonial era that subjugated over ninety percent of the Muslim world to Western political dominance only opened fresh wounds. To be sure, accusations can fly in many directions. Islam too harbors its own evil history. But that hardly cancels out ours. The pinnacle of Western madness, the Holocaust, still leaves us stunned and the church not undefiled. New pinnacles of madness haunt us ever afresh—nuclear devastation, ecological imbalance, the list is just beginning.

Whether it be Africa, the Indian subcontinent, the islands of the Pacific, the Americas, or East Asia, home to a third of the world's people, the story of Western oppression has been the same. Although the church and the Western nation-states are far from coterminus, in the recent past the two, building upon a Constantinian foundation, have too often been co-workers. Western hegemony has brought both blight and blessing. We don't like to consider blight; we prefer to recount the blessings.

The world interrogates the church. Where were you in all this? Is this what it means for the church to be "for others"? Is this how the church goes public? This interrogation raises the first great question that Christian mission must answer worldwide today. That question is, "Why the church?" It is forced upon us because the church as an institution has proved in many instances to be as oppressive as many other institutions and has been implicated in some of the greatest tragedies of history. We might think it is a stupid question, but those outside the church do not. The inescapable question, and one of the first we must face, is not how the world is a problem for us, but how we, the church, have become a problem for the world.

Perhaps the institutional church as we now know it is dispensable. But the solution is not that simple. For this is the only human institution grounded consciously upon the story of Jesus. For this reason, the question about the church leads directly to the deepest theological question of all. The world, other religions, perversely, we might think, ask, "Why Jesus?" or, to make the question sting even more, "Why the Jesus you preach?" This is the second great question the witnessing church must address. We have, whether we wanted to or not, implicated God, the God of Covenant, the God of Jesus, in our history. We have cast aspersion on the gospel because of our deeds. Our supposed faith leads others to fault God. The tragedy of the contemporary church is great indeed!

A Venturesome Circle?

It is only in the midst of the struggle that we will experience grace. From failed work we go back to sure word, and then to work again. If dialogue requires venture, then participation does so even more. Yet, what about this still another circle—from failed work to word, and back to work? Is the circle venturesome?

We close with two preliminary suggestions: transparency and anticipation.

Transparency: Each of those five circles we have spoken of need to be transparent to the others. Similarly those modes of witness we discussed—worship, evangelism, dialogue, participation—also need to be transparent to each other. Like transparencies on an overhead projector, the design on each coordinates with the design of each of the others. Only when all are placed together does the full picture appear.

The point is simple enough. Economic values, for example, cannot run roughshod over ecological values. On the other hand, genuine ecological values are open to the needs of justice and nurture. Simplicity is not its own end. And all of these circles are transparent, for the Christian community, to the modes of witness, just as the modes of witness are open to these varied circles.

Worship, evangelism, dialogue, and participation form a single whole. None stands alone. Surely it was the case with Jesus that each of these spheres was open to all the others. Indeed, the transparency between Jesus, his word and work, and God was of such a nature that it could only be spoken of as incarnation. "My food is to do the will of him who sent me" (John 4:34, cf. 5:30). "I and the Father are one" (John 10:30). "We have beheld his glory, glory as of the only Son from the Father" (John 1:14). Embedded in all these spheres and modes was the cruciform. Transparency to this word and work into which we have been baptized is the conformity with Christ that we covet.

Anticipation: The Christian community in all its endeavors lives by anticipation. We anticipate a coming kingdom, a kingdom that is already with us. We anticipate a future when all things shall be subjected to God, who even now reigns. We anticipate a future in which nothing shall separate us from the love of God, whose love is already sure.

Anticipation is a state of mind; even more, it is an action. We anticipate the future by doing today what the future promises for tomorrow. This is to live by hope and faith. Our work is anticipatory; it is not final. We do not bring about the kingdom; we anticipate the kingdom. The kingdom has already come as prelude in Jesus. These anticipations are always fragmentary, always ambiguous, but they are anticipations. To the degree our participation in the world as a Christian community is transparent to God's cruciform, behind it our work is anticipation.

What then do we do, given all of the above? We worship, we evangelize, we dialogue, we participate. We can do nothing less; we can do nothing more. Doing all four, the circle becomes venturesome.

Notes

1. "The Augsburg Confession," Article 7, in *The Book of Concord,* trans. and ed. Theodore G. Tappert (Philadelphia: Fortress Press, 1972), 32.

2. Ibid., 173, from "Apology to the Augsburg Confession," Articles 7-8.
3. I refer here to Karl Jasper's notion of "the axial age"—a time in which a fundamental reorientation took place in these regions of the world in understanding the place of the human within the cosmos. He placed this period roughly between 800-200 B.C.E. In the Middle East he had in mind particularly the prophetic movement in Israel. See his *The Origin and Goal of History*, trans. Michael Bullock (New Haven: Yale University Press, 1953).
4. Above we seemed to distinguish worship from witness. That was only to emphasize the inward aspect of worship and the outward aspect of witness. It should be clear from our discussion that the purpose of worship is to adore and praise God. Witness is a natural consequence of worship as worship is a necessary presupposition of witness.
5. We do not add "evil" here because God alone, not the church, is the final arbiter of who or what is evil. The church itself is a mixture of wheat and tares.
6. For one brief guide in this area see *Counsel for Lutherans With Respect to Interfaith Worship* (LCUSA/Division of Theological Studies, 1986). For a fuller discussion of worship see Eugene L. Brand, *Worship Among Lutherans* (Geneva: Lutheran World Federation, 1983). Note especially the discussion of norms and worship and mission, 21-23.
7. James Scherer, *That the Gospel May Be Sincerely Preached Throughout the World*: A Lutheran Perspective on Mission and Evangelism in the 20th Century (Geneva: LWF Report, 1982), 183.
8. Ibid., 250.
9. Clifford Geertz, *The Interpretation of Cultures* (New York: Basic Books, 1973), 5.
10. Paul Tillich, *A Theology of Culture*, ed. Robert C. Kimball (New York: Oxford University Press, 1959), 42.